D1156721

A
Dowagiac
Collection

WHERE IT STARTED -- Dowagiac had its beginning at the old Upper Mill, built in 1833 and razed in 1948. The mills brought roads and settlers to this community. Painting by Lionel L. Vanderburg.

This book is dedicated to the memory
of my late husband, Lionel L.
Vanderburg, whose idea it was, and
to my very supportive family.

To:
Berenice E. Vanderburg, for her many years of service as Secretary of the Cass County Historical Society, we respectfully dedicate this second printing of "A Dowagiac Collection."

A Dowagiac Collection

This is just what the title says it is--a collection of Dowagiac stories, gathered from old newpapers, old time residents now gone, and my own research through the over 45 years on the news staff of The Dowagiac Daily News.

It is not an orthodox book, I am merely trying to preserve some of Dowagiac's interesting and fascinating history, and give you a taste and flavor of a Dowagiac that used to be. As you read some of these stories, you will come to realize that it was not a typical small town. Today it has become more standardized as has everything else, yet something of that old time atmosphere still lingers.

I want to emphasize that while this book is historical in nature, it is not a history of Dowagiac, it is for from complete. There is so much more to be researched and written about but I wouldn't live long enough to do it.

Because this is primarily from newspapers, I want to point out that newspapers are the greatest source of history there is, every day they record some aspect of what becomes history, whether it was last week or 100 years ago.

Many of you have already read these stories from special editions and features, but unless you hung on to old newspapers you have lost them. Also I am happy to know of at least two people who are preparing to expand in detail two of the subjects I have written about.

Our earliest newspapers are missing and the oldest known ones from Dowagiac known to be in existence, is the old Dowagiac Republican. The files from about 1860 to 1864 are in the Burton section of the Detroit Public Library. The Daily News has files going back to 1874 and pretty complete since then. The Daily News itself, Feb. 6, 1897 was the first issue, is on Microfilm at the Dowagiac Library.

I appreciate all the help I have had through the years and so much has been told to me by people who are all gone. At the time I was not experienced enough to realize I should have been jotting down my sources, but I will give them, if i know them, as I go along.

Cass County is equally as interesting, but I confined myself to Dowagiac. although I did step outside the city limits once or twice.

Again I want to thank everyone who have been so much help to me. And please note that the story of The Dowagiac Diamond, Michigan's only diamond, is by John Gillette, owner of Hardscrabble Books, and publisher of my book. I asked him to do it. After all he is the great-grandson of Isaac Wells Sr. who found the diamond, and a former president of The Historical Society of Michigan. In recent years he has become a newspaper man, owning the Berrien Journal Era and the Bridgman Enterprise.

I hope you will enjoy this book as much as I did in writing it.

Table of Contents

Glacial Lake	11
Dowagiac's Origins	13
How Dowagiac Started	18
Indian Land	21
Dowagiac's Name	24
Had Two Faces	27
A Real Puzzle	30
Early Stores	32
The Spaulding Store	35
A Spaulding Letter	37
The Wigwam	41
Newspapers	43
The First Telephone	45
The Automobile	49
Beckwith Theater	54
The Early Years	58
The Round Oak	60
The Round Oak Range	64
The Round Oak Whistle	66
P.D. Beckwith	68
Farm Implements Made	70
The Heddons	75
Oldest Public Building	83
First Schools	85
First School Board	88
High School	90
High School Graduation	94
The Bible	96
Dowagiac Churches	97
Ladies Library Association	99

Fire Department 101
Fire Department Organized 106
Fire Stories 110
First Fairs 113
The Beardless Band 115
First Orphan Train 117
Fourth of July 122
The Dowagiac Diamond 125
The Civil War 128
Organized in Dowagiac 132
Company E 133
Dead Man's Hollow 136
Civil War Incidents 141
Custer 144
The Clarke Brothers 148
Some Firsts 150
Citizens of Dowagiac 151
Renesten 154
Nicholas Bock 157
Justus Gage 159
Patrick Hamilton 161
The Hamiltons 163
Noahdia Potter 166
Daniel McOmber 167
H.B. Tuthill 169
King Gillette 178
Flavia Defendorf 184
Florence Cushman Milner 189
Frances Willard 202
Doctor McMaster 203
Abner Moon 205
Abner Moon Stories 207
Simon Pokagon 210

Dowagiac's Biggest Man   211
Stephen Topash   213
That Other Side   215
How It Was   218

1

Glacial Lake

This entire area was once covered by a glacial lake which geologists have named "Lake Dowagiac." The lake, about ten miles across, stretched north to what is now Grand Rapids, south to the vicinity of South Bend.

The late George R. Fox, historian and archaeologist, took members of the Cass County Historical Society on a glacial site tour. The group drove to a point two miles northeast of what was his home, "Wilderness Farm" on the Rudy Road to a hill where a clear view could be obtained of the valley once covered by the glacial Lake Dowagiac. This lake was open when Lakes Michigan and Huron were frozen over during one of the ice ages.

The city of Dowagiac, said Mr. Fox, lies in the center of the lake bed on the lowest or "deepest" part of this area,

In the distance could be seen the hills which marked the lake's western boundaries by the group which was standing on its eastern "shores."

The lake was the drainage point for rivers of Michigan on both the east and west sides of the state as well as most of the Great Lakes.

The late Grover Kimmerle of Cassopolis, some years ago found a book in South Bend describing this lake or river which it said reached from the bluffs just west of Niles, east to a range of hills east of Beebe's marsh land, and that all the water from as far north as Grand Rapids passed down through this Dowagiac or "Dowagiake" River as the name appeared on early maps, and which was in reality a long, wide lake, and on down through what is now the Kankakee River bed in Indiana to Illinois.

The article further stated that the "fall was some 31 feet, greater fall in the landscape west of Niles than there was between South Bend and Niles." And that in high water times the water got to seeping through these bluffs deep enough so that the Dowagiac River turned off at this point and ran down into Lake Michigan emptying at what is now Benton Harbor and St. Joseph.

"This caused the river to reverse itself and run from South Bend to Niles rather than from Niles to South Bend." It was said that the two little lakes at Notre Dame and St. Mary's are practically all that is left "of this great inland lake or river."

2

Dowagiac's Origins

How Dowagiac happened to be here is a combination of natural and man made features. As remarked once before, Dowagiac did not emerge full grown from one of those old funnel-shaped smokestacks of the Michigan Central -- it was already here -- just waiting to be named.

The Dowagiac Creek really gave the city its start, just be being here, because in 1830 it provided William Renesten with water power to establish his carding mill -- 18 years before the arrival of the railroad. Renesten dammed the creek in 1832 to create The Dowagiac Millpond, on which he built his grist mill in 1833. Roads were built to "Renesten's carding mill;" Dennis Wright built a sawmill in 1834, and settlers moved in needing to be as close to the mills as possible.

Another contributing factor was the Grand River Indian Trail which linked Kalamazoo with the Carey Mission in what is now Niles and settlers were inclined to follow Indian trails. After centuries the Indian knew pretty well the best places to travel. In 1834 the government surveyed a road over this trail and by 1836 stagecoaches were traveling over it.

Land seekers were flocking into Michigan, helped by the building of the Erie Canal in New York, and as one time as high as 50 stagecoahces a day passed through here.

Occasionally stagecoach drivers would turn off the road here just to provide his weary passengers with a few laughs at the expense of this crude little hamlet.

The trail came through Volinia and Wayne Townships, down over Henderson Hill, and west over what is now Prairie Ronde Street, down in the vicinity of North Front and turned off toward what is now M-51.

Soon after the stagecoach line was established, James McOmber built his tavern at the corner of what is now North Front and Prairie Ronde, where a grocery store is now located. This was a famous tavern in its day and no more distinguished than its proprietor, James McOmber. Country dances were held in this building and pioneers for miles around flocked to attend. He had a small store in one corner of the tavern and this was a great aid to the settlers.

It was reported that in 1842 the entire population of Dowagiac lived in four log cabins in what is now Dowagiac. But there were people coming in constantly, since it had had a school since 1840.

When the news of the coming of the railroad reached the ears of Jacob Beeson and Nicholas Cheesebrough of Niles, they bought land of Patrick Hamilton, who had come here in 1835, and began platting the village. The plat was recorded Feb. 16, 1848, and in September of that same year, the first little Michigan Central train puffed into Dowagiac.

The coming of the railroad made a tremendous difference, its influence was felt even before the tracks were complete here. The little village literally burst at the seams.

By 1860 Dowagiac was the largest wheat shpping station on the Michigan Central and into the 1870's before the western wheat fields opened up. There was a time in the very early days when it shipping was greater than that of Chicago.

On "wheat days," farmers were lined up for blocks waiting to unload their grain, which often took hours, almost a whole day. Farmers often found themselves talking to other farmers, whose homes were 50 miles from each other. They came in from Pipestone, Bainbridge, Keeler, Hamilton, Decatur, and all points east, west, north and south.

Pioneers who had to travel through the dread Dowagiac swamp to reach the shipping here, waited until their neighbors were ready to go too and literally traveled in small caravans. My husband's grandfather, William Summerell of Bainbridge Township, near Watervliet, brought his wheat to Dowagiac a distance of almost 20 miles. He was a strong brave man, but he too went with a group of neighbors through the swamp, which was in those days much larger and wilder in character.

The swamp had an evil reputation which pioneers said harbored robbers and horse thieves. An occasional body was found there -- usually someone unknown in the community.

At the same time Dowagiac was also a big stock shipping station. In those days there were no Chicago facilities for handling live hogs, and the old freight house here in the winter would be piled high with the frozen carcasses of hogs, awaiting shipment. Dowagiac for many years had its own stockyards beside the railroad, and local residents used to complain about the odor.

It was intended by the town planners that Main Street be the principal street and for that reason was designed wider than the other streets in the original plat. But early business men ignored it. Everyone wanted to be near the railroad so they built along Front Street and that's how it is today.

The fact that Dowagiac has a "High Street," bespeaks its New England heritage. Some street names have been changed, there used to be a Green Street all over town according to the old 1872 plat map. In recent years, Ohio Street was officially closed, although no one could ever remember when it had been in existence. The Lee Memorial Hospital grounds occupy it.

Dowagiac's shortest street, Pine Street, was also officially wiped off the map in recent years, after the Ladies Library Association building was razed. It ran beside the Beery Pharmacy building and a great many people sitll use it.

Dowagiac was not incorporated as a village until 1858, and in the first village election held in Nicholas Bock's American House, Justus Gage was elected the first village president.

In 1877 when Dowagiac became a city, it was then the smallest incorporated city in the United States. Attorney Freeman J. Atwell was the first mayor.

In the beginning Dowagiac was as about an ugly little hamlet as could be imagined, its wooden shacks and log houses set down in oak grubs and sand. Its residents were so busy trying to get a toehold that esthetic considerations were far from their minds.

When Sarah Clarke Lippincott came here in 1858 to visit her brother, Attorney Joseph Clarke, she was shocked by its appearance. She was a well known writer in her day, using the name, "Grace Greenwood" and belonged to the coterie of New England poets and writers which included Whittier and others. She wrote a description of Dowagiac to a Philadelphia newspaper, which fell into the hands of local residents. She said there wasn't enough grass "on which to bleach a handkerchief."

That stung the pride of the village fathers and right away they got busy, paying 50 cents apiece to have stumps removed from Front Street and other principal streets. Shade trees and grass were planted and soon Dowagiac outgrew its ugly duckling stage.

In 1861 the principal business block lay between Main and Commercial Streets on the west side of Front Street, consisting of a number of wooden buildings. On each side of Commercial Street were a few wooden buildings, and three or four on the east side of Front Street north of Beeson Street. There was one brick building on Front Street. The other brick building in Dowagiac was the ReShore house still standing on West Division Street. There were also some wooden buildings on Front between Commercial and Division, some of which were destroyed in a fire in the 1850's.

During the Civil War the two big fires of 1864 and 1865 destroyed most of these wooden buildings. And nearly all of the brick buildings which rose up in their places are still here today. During the Civil War the east side of Front Street and the park were nothing but sandpiles.

Only a small portion of the city was settled and thick woods surrounded the little hamlet. It was said there was but one house on North Front Street to Prairie Ronde Street.

What is now the Fair Store faced Beeson Street and the city prison was located north of it.

But Dowagiac already had a high school, a frame two story-building which stood in the woods where Central Junior High School is situated today. It was not very thickly settled although this was a part of the original part of Dowagiac.

Down on Pennsylvania Avenue near the waterworks was a

distillery where Benjamin Cooper manufactured wines. The old brewery on Cass Avenue was also doing a good business.

Bolivar Poore had a blacksmith shop at the corner of Spruce and Lowe Streets, and a wagon and carriage shop stood on the site of Mrs. F.L. Harden's home on Green and West Division Streets.

Horace Jones and Peter Hannan had a basket factory at Park Place. There were three hotels. The American House operated by Nicholas Bock at the corner of Front and West Division; the Exchange Hotel on South Front Street; and the old Bannard Hotel on Beeson Street. The post office was on Commercial Street in the building occupied by the Dowagiac Pastry Shop until it was recently razed. The old Michigan Central Depot was said to be a few rods north of its present location, although the 1872 plat map of Dowagiac shows it to be south of it near the corner of Park Place.

P.D. Beckwith was busy operating his foundry beside the creek on South Front Street.

One of the very earliest descriptions of what is now Dowagiac, came from Isaac Wells Sr. of Dowagiac. He was celebrating his 70th birthday in 1900 and told of making a trip through Dowagiac in 1841.

He said there were but four houses. At the northern terminus of what is now Center Street, stood a house occupied by Patrick Hamilton; Daniel McOmber lived on the corner of North Front and Prairie Ronde Streets "adjoining the Catholic Cemetery. Frances McOmber Brizendine said her grandfather told her there was once an Indian burial ground on his property, and probably still is.

Francis Mosher "lived across the present railroad track on the high bank opposite the Drill Works. The fourth house was the Watson place near the Middle Crossing, and owned by Charles Avery in 1900. The Daniel McOmber home was a tavern and stage stop as there were people living in the community outside of what is now Dowagiac. Also there was a school here at that time.

3

How Dowagiac Started

The mills were responsible for Dowagiac's beginning. The first white settlers had come to Cass County just five years before, 1825, when William Renesten came up from southern Indiana with his milling equipment and built his carding mill on the banks of the Dowagiac Creek, only a few rods outside the present Dowagiac city limits.

In 1833 he built a grist mill. The year before he had dammed up the Dowagiac Creek which created the present Dowagiac Millpond. Settlers naturally wanted to be near the mills, as about the same time Dennis Wright had built a sawmill beside the pond too. Justus Gage, who came to Wayne Township in 1837, mentioned in his memoirs of passing the little settlement along the dam.

The site of the first dam was pointed out to me some years ago by the late Dr. Jesse Ritter, a great-grandson of William Renesten, who had shown it to him. There is a depression in the ground on the south side of the present highway below Old Mill Farm. This was it.

That first grist mill, known in later years as the "Upper Mill," torn down in 1948, was the nucleus of a milling business that has gone on without interruption since 1833.

The Mennel Company, is the successor to the Dowagiac Milling Company, and has greatly expended the business since taking over. The company which is based in Fostoria, Ohio, is headed by Don M. Mennel, who is the fourth generation Mennel to serve as its president.

In 1857 Gilbert Colby started a flouring mill on the site of the present Mennel Mill, which he later sold to his brother, H.F. Colby, and moved to Niles. In 1868 H.F. Colby purchased the old Spalding mill and the two mills were operated as one business from that time on until the old Upper Mill went out of existence. The Mill Street mill was always known as the "Lower Mill." Owners gave them fancier names but local residents never called them by anything else.

There are many pictures of the old "Upper Mill," which is not surprising. "The American Miller," a national magazine, once reported that it was one of the most photographed mills in America.

The Judd Lumber Company and Phillipson's Clothing Store are two of the oldest businesses, both originating in 1858. Richard M. Judd Jr. is the fifth generation Judd in the business which began life as a planing mill.

There were four generations of Phillipsons involved with the local store, now headed by Irving Phillipson.

The I. Oppenheim Store is another business well over a century old and also family operated. The clothing store was opened in 1874 by Mark Oppenheim who later sold his interest to his brothers, Israel and Ben. It is now owned and operated by Maurice Oppenheim, son of Israel.

The Beery Pharmacy is another business that has seen more than a century. It was established in 1868 as the C.L. Sherwood Drug Store. It was located further south on Front Street. The present store building was erected in 1885.

He later took in Ray Burlingame as a partner, and it was Sherwood and Burlingame for years; then Burlingame and Stahl, and after other owners, to its present ownership.

I have not gone into the history of these businesses as I feel it should be done in much more detail than I could do.

Some of the early factories here included the manufacture of the Pitt threshing machine by John Crawford and Dr. George W. Fosdick; and the Davis Machine Shop, 1850, purchased by P.D. Beckwith in 1854; Daniel Lyle's shore factory (1850); 1857 the basket factory which moved to Chicago in 1878; the Round Oak; the Dowagiac Manufacturing Co. in 1865 and James Heddon's bait factory.

It was the coming of the railroad in 1848 that made a boom town out of Dowagiac. People came in so fast that housing was scarce. It was not incorporated until 1858 when Justus Gage was elected its first president. But it had a high school in 1857 and that no doubt was due to its New England heritage. Education was important to our early residents.

4

Indian Land

Dowagiac's history did not begin with the arrival of the first white man -- it began here thousands of years ago and its origin is lost in the mists of time.

This land was the Indian's and the white man is the usurper. Two hundred years is but a fleeting moment in this area's history.

To quote the late George R. Fox, well known archaelogist and local resident: "Cass County is that part of Michigan that first became habitable on the melting away of the glacial ice sheet. It is part of the great recession of glaciers which stretched north from the Michigan-Indiana line to Kent County and from the solidly frozen Lake Michigan at the east Berrien County line to the ice of the then Lake Huron in Washtenaw County.

"The first men in Michigan invaded this recession area some 10,000 to 30,000 years ago. Their weapons, the Folsom, or fluted type of point and those of the Sandia man, the single-shouldered type, are found scattered all over this county through the surface soil above the glacial deposit. As these primitives did in the far west, these men of Cass probably hunted the mammoth. These huge elephants roamed over Cass County; at least eight skeletal remains of these creatures have been found here in the marl pits.

"In the days before settlement by the white man, Cass County was well populated. More than 25 Indian mounds were found in the county. The pioneers found Indian garden beds on every prairie and in every township.

"French trappers visited the county long before any permanent settlement was made. LaSalle crossed the county on one of his trips across Michigan.

"Three bands of Potawatomis occupied the county when the first settlers came. Weesaw's band of 150 members had their winter camp in Newton's Woods; Shavehead's band of about 75 had their main camp about three miles east of Shavehead Lake; and Pokagon with 250, had a summer camp and cornfield on the Pokagon prairie in the township that bears his name."

Cass County was a network of Indian trails, one of them, the Grand River Indian Trail, passing through what is now Dowagiac. Porter Township seemed to have the most trails. Many main Indian thoroughfares passed through Cass County, north and south and east and west, including the Sauk trail which was part of the main trail between the Atlantic and the Pacific.

In 1825 when the first white settlers came there were a dozen Indian villages in Cass and Berrien Counties, and at least 100 different locations during the first 25 years of the 1800's, the most important ones being located on the St. Joseph River.

It is said that Cass County had 42 mounds, of which 14 are still visible, and dating back to the Hopewell culture. These Indians were very intelligent and highly artistic as evidenced by the artifacts they left behind.

George Fox found 13 Indian trails still visible in Cass County, that is portions of them. M-51 South still follows the Grand River Indian Trail in many places.

The white settlers greed for land caused the government to coerce or even force the Indians to sell their lands at prices way below their value and move to reservations in the west.

The government reneged on its payments and for more than a century local Indians and Indians everywhere are still fighting for their rights -- and now are putting up a successful fight to save their own heritage. Some are being repaid and the Potawatomi Indians in this area are hopeful of some day receiving their rightful dues.

Sentiment has gradually changed in their favor and many of their white brethren are trying to help them realize their ambitions.

This area now has the Southwestern Michigan Indian Center at Watervliet headed by Joseph Winchester of Sister Lakes, and

Dowagiac has an Indian Parents Club, all testifying that the Indian is once more becoming proud of his ancient heritage and working to preserve it.

5

Dowagiac's Name

Very few cities in the United States are more "harassed" by its name than Dowagiac. It is spelled, or rather mispelled in every possible and impossible way. Even its origin is subject to various interpretations.

As early as 1855, Lippincott's Pronouncing Gazeteer of the World, gave the population of Dowagiac in 1853 at 300, (in 1855 it was 608) and described it as a "post village on the Do-wa-je-ak River and on the Michigan Central."

Another old story told over and over again in various newspapers, was some years ago printed in The Detroit Free Press's Town Crier column. "Spelling: Boss Man McKee of the Michigan Central was dictating a note to his superintendent, who was coming over from Chicago to meet him. 'Tell him' said McKee, 'to meet me in Dowagiac.' The secretary paused in her note-taking. 'Mr. McKee,' she ventured, 'how do you spell Dowagiac?' McKee stared at her a moment, 'Dowagiac? O hell, tell him I'll meet him in Niles and we'll drive over!"

The name is of course of Indian origin. The late Michael Williams of Niles, who was a native of Silver Creek, and for many years chairman of the Potawatomi Indians of Indiana and Michigan, Inc. explained where the name came from some years before his death.

He said the name came from the Potwatomi word, "Ndowagayuk," which means "foraging ground" as near as he could translate it. He said:

"Old timers who, or whose parents may have been early enough in time to have seen this region in its virgin glory must have reveled in its richness and affluence of material things, a region stupendous in richness, abundance and variety. Realm of the famed Dowagiac swamp.

"Here in this region the native Indians could find anything they wanted or needed, anytime, anywhere. Here in this area was plentiful game to be had in all seasons; here were luscious fruits and berries in variety; and here were life-sustaining vegetables, greens, and grains -- any of which the natives could gather and use for food.

"And here were bushes, plants, grasses, barks, herbs, to concoct their remedies. In fine, when they needed anything for food, for medicine, or materials for their garments, it was to be had here in quantities and qualities. It was becauseof this over-all plentiude of all things here that the Potawatomi called this region, 'Ndowagayuk.' A fitting translation of the word could have been 'foraging ground.' "

Mr. Williams went on to say that he used the word "guardedly" not intending it to mean the foraging forays by soldiers in ancient times who lived off the land and people around them. "Ndowagayuk itself, in more detail, means an area in which to hunt; to look, probe or prod for, to get.

"Your D O W A G I A C would not be too far deviated from the Potawatomi 'ndowagayuk' if you give the consonant 'g' the hard sound and the vowel 'i' the sound of the diphthong 'i' to educe dowagi, and the final syllable unaccented, you would almost have ndowagayuk. At least it would sound near enough like it so any Potawatomi would know what you are trying to say -- if he himself knows. And that probably is what the godparents wanted it to be in the first place."

The godparents in this case were Michigan Central officials who named the little hamlet when they placed a depot here. They spelled it "by ear." However long before this, some very old maps called it the "Dowagiake River."

Justus Gage in his memoirs of 1837, told it this way in speaking of the Dowagiac River. "The Indian name of the river, 'Da-wa-ga-awk' with the 'a' broad all the way through, and in their gutteral pronunciation thrown into two syllables with a slight quaver to denote the others, was as yet unutterable by the white settlers, and remained so until the MCRR Co. brought it into English, and gave the name of the river to their station at the crossing of the creek, and which has now become the euphonious name, as well of the beautiful village of 'Do-wa-giac.' "

6

Had Two Faces

Dowagiac had two "faces" in the early days, due to the type of pioneers who settled here. There were the cultured New Englanders and the more rough and ready. But somehow they managed to weld a village and a community of which they could be proud.

The railroad brought all kinds of people here, many of them land speculators and out to make a fast buck -- others were here to seek their fortunes and make a better life for themselves.

With her rows of wooden buildings, the old Blue Ruin saloon on Beeson Street and the Red Ruin across the way, and liquor sold over hotel bars and many other places, Dowagiac resembled nothing more than an old mining town in the west -- except that this was the western frontier.

Whiskey was as plentiful as milk, "and a whole lot cheaper," reported one old timer. It sold for three cents a dipperful, and a few dipperfuls were sure to bring on a fight. The thirsty one usually stepped up and asked for some of "The Critter," or "Old Budge," but it was whiskey, no matter what it was called.

It has been vouched for that Dowagiac at one time had 16 saloons -- but was forced to cut down to ten due to a state law. At any rate there were ten in existence in 1899. It must be remembered that in those days saloons were almost all confined to the urban areas, unless it might have been the "Red Onion" out somewhere in the wilds of Wayne Township. Today taverns are scattered throughout rural areas due to fast transportation that didn't exist here in the early days. The big night in Dowagiac was Saturday night, when streets were so crowded that it was difficult to get through at times.

Farmers came from miles around to do their trading, usually coming in during the day and remaining during the evening hours. If the truth is known, they came mainly for sociability and a chance to visit with friends and neighbors. Hitching posts and rails lined many of the streets, and fortunately for many, the horses knew their way home.

But Dowagiac had many pioneers with a deep sense of responsibility, and in due course of time, took over, most of the shysters and speculators drifting off to greener fields. But enough of the rougher element remained so that every Saturday night could be counted upon for a few good fights, the participants being hauled off to the old jail on Beeson Street to cool off and sober up.

For the more responsible segment of society, church-going was the principal form of entertainment in the very early days. While church-going was regarded as a serious duty, it also provided its lighter side. Singing in the choir meant a chance to go to singing schools in the winter time and these were highly popular. Many were hungry for the culture they had left behind.

Taverns usually devoted their second floors to dance halls and the young and vigorous pioneer often danced until dawn. Good fiddlers and callers were always in demand and never out of a job. The pioneers worked hard and earned their pleasures.

The custom of afternoon tea was started here early, and a regular institution. With no sidewalks or street lights, it was a difficult matter to be out after dark.

Dowagiac residents made improving their minds a serious matter and a duty. There were lecture series and the speaker was always greeted by capacity audiences. Many who came here were talented people and could entertain with music, readings, etc. Spelling matches were most popular as were debates. Theatrical companies came and played in Young Men's Hall over the present Phillipson Store. Many a rousing political rally was held here, and Thomas Jefferson played in "Rip Van Winkle," then one of the most noted actors of his day. Indian medicine shows and circuses also provided the pioneer a respite from his labors.

The Universalist Church provided the town with its lecture

platform and here famous speakers of their day could be heard, Susan B. Anthony, Sojourner Truth and others.

There were the old Dowagaic Union Fairs which brought thousands to Dowagaic; sleigh rides and oyster suppers. And as always, women were always raising money to buy carpeting for the church or repair the church roof, with maple sugar festivals, ice cream socials, strawberry festivals, and the always popular church suppers.

Croquet was very popular here more than a century ago, and Dowagiac had several star roque players, roque being a game similar to croquet. And the bicycle took the town by storm and many were lectured severely for "scorching" on the city streets. Baseball was played everywhere and every little four corners had its team and rivalry was intense.

The horse was as important to the old time resident as the automobile is today, and horse racing was apt to take place on any Dowagiac street as well as on the local race track. Snow racing was a popular sport with Prairie Ronde Street, the race track. Many old barns are still in evidence in the older parts of Dowagiac, and all converted into garages. The death of a horse was apt to be reported in the weekly newspaper -- it was a serious matter.

A custom that has long since fallen into disuse was the New Year's Day calls. Weekly newspapers carried notices that certain young ladies would be receiving, and young men of the village donned their best "bibs and tuckers" and made the rounds. Married women often received too and their friends would call, sometimes two or three hostesses going together to entertain at one house. It was a gracious custom and one that ought to be revived. It was a pleasant way of life, when people made their own fun, worked hard for what they had -- and a way of life that is gone forever.

7

A Real Puzzle

How to find your way around Dowagiac, small as it is, can be a problem to a stranger. An economic survey made here about 30 years ago, said the basic street pattern was affected by four major forces -- the railroad, the street pattern of the first village plat, the street pattern around the original plat, and the Dowagiac Creek.

Then add on Dowagiac's Philadelphia numbering system for its houses, which I won't attempt to explain, the puzzle is complete. However old time residents here are rather proud of Dowagiac's uniqueness in this respect. We know where we are.

Years ago an old time newspaperman decided to be helpful. He said: "The railroad was responsible for the diagonal directions of the streets in the business portion of the city. In the words of the plat, 'Front Street runs parallel to the track of the Michigan Central Railroad.'

"The Railroad runs at an angle of 36 degrees with the north and south line. Hence to get north bearings when standing on Front Street it is necessary to face about two-fifths of a right angle.

"The calculation and sense of direction needed to perform this feat properly are greater than most citizens will practice, and only the oldest residents can figure out the time of day by the position of the sun and reduce the bizarre directions to the four fundamentals of the sign post."

To get back to the modern reasons for Dowagiac's crazy quilt streets, as someone once described them, the railroad started it all. "It runs at a diagonal to the city's square outline and encourages location of industry along the diagonal. In so doing it divided residential development into two distinct major sections, and acts as a disrupter of street traffic and city pattern."

The survey pointed out that Jacob Beeson and Nicholas Cheeseborough who platted the village, used the railroad as the basic line for all streets. Subsequent subdividers used section and township lines, which were probably easier to survey.

There are also several bridge crossings in the city over the Dowagiac Creek which also are restrictive as railroad crossings said the survey.

"The city's street pattern was established before the Civil War and before the automobile."

8

Early Stores

There were stores of a sort or "stocks of goods" rather, before the coming of the Michigan Central Railroad in 1848, as this area was being rapidly settled. There was enough people around here to establish a school in what is now Dowagiac in 1840. James McOmber kept a store or at least some items pioneers needed in is tavern at the corner of North Front and Prairie Ronde Street on what was once the Grand River Indian Trail. This was in the 1840's.

Abner Moon in his history of Dowagiac said that in the winter of 1847-48 two men by the name of Kendall and Phetteplace opened a store in a part of the Ira Mosher house then located at what is now 212 E. High St. They were building the new freight house and sold goods mainly to the men working there.

They were followed by Arad C. Balch, Dowagiac's first postmaster, who opened up a small "stock of goods" in the "Cataract House," a boarding house standing on the bluff just east of the railroad tracks, probably on what is now Park Place. He kept the post office there for a short time.

Joel H. Smith who had been in business in Cassopolis with his brother, Ezekiel Smith, came to the city. He and his brother built a building on the corner of Front and Main Streets, afterwards known as the Foster building. It was the first structure built in Dowagiac for that purpose.

This building was later purchased by Edwin Pattison, who moved it to Indian Lake and converted it into a barn "in connection with his summer outings."

"The stock of goods for the Smith store was hauled here by a team from Cassopolis in February, 1848, the month in which Dowagiac's first plat was recorded by Jacob Beeson, by Ezekiel Smith and M.T. Garvey. They arrived after dark, and had much trouble in locating the building as the virgin forest still covered the ground, not a tree having been cut in the streets." There were streets laid out on the plat but actually no trace of them had yet come into existence.

"They slept in the store that night, and the next morning Mr. Smith went to Patrick Hamilton's for breakfast. (Patrick Hamilton's farm home was located at what is now West Telegraph at the end of Center Street), while Mr. Garvey found a boarding place with a carpenter who was working on the freight house. As Mr. Garvey stepped out of the store that morning he looked in vain to find a house, but nothing but trees and grubs met his gaze except the freight house, and he remarked to Mr. Smith that it didn't look much like a town. Mr. Smith replied it would be a town some day -- a prophecy that has been more than fulfilled, although it took a stretch of imagination to see it then."

In 1850 Joshua Lofland built a large brick store at what is now 214 S. Front Street, and in this building Lofland, Henley C. Lybrook and Gilman C. Jones began a general mercantile business. Lybrook sold out after five years to his partners.

Ballengee, Wagner & Co. began business in 1851, and there was a rush of people to go into business into Dowagiac which was growing fast. Wells Atwood bought out Joel Smith's interest; Incidentally the brick building built by Joshua Lofland, burned in 1866. Tuthill & Sturgis, H.E. Ellis, Becraft and Bowling, and A. Van Uxem came, all in 1851, and Gideon Gibbs and Abram Townsend started selling groceries the same year. Azro Jones and Horace Jones joined G.C. Jones.

Histories say that Jacob Hirsch began selling clothing here in 1850. His brother-in-law, Emmanuel Phillipson joined him later, and Hirsch went to Chicago and became a well known merchant there.

The first drug store was conducted by Asa Huntington who came here in 1852 and had his store where the Masonic Temple is now located. He was followed by N.B. Hollister.

The first hardware store was conducted by J.C. and George

Andrew beginning in the year, 1850 in the basement of Nickolas Bock's American House on the corner of Division and Front Streets. J.C. Andrew sold out to his brother who eventually built on West Division Street.

The names come thick and fast, Benjamin Cooper and Francis J. Mosher who had the first store specializing mainly in groceries; Theodore Stebbins and A.G. Ramsay (the latter an ancestor of Dr. Robert Neff) began selling groceries in 1857. Other grocers included Louis ReShore, a native of France, Carl Gerding, L. Brewer & Co. Henry and Fred Lee, W.D. Jones, Azro Jones, Adams & Hopkins, Jacob Sturr and G.I. Peck.

F.G. Larzelere & Co. (the company was Daniel Larzelere and a man named Babbitt) established a dry goods store in 1855 which was operated for 12 years when it was sold to Archibald Jewell & Co.

The Oppenheim Brothers opened their dry goods and clothing store in 1871 and Maurice Oppenheim still carries on the Oppenheim business.

9

The Spaulding Store

Histories fail to mention one of Dowagiac's first stores -- a general store built north of Beeson Street near the railroad tracks by Erastus Holmes Spalding and a man by the ame of Starkweather. Spalding later became a mill operator.

The old day book, owned by the late Dr. Harold Spalding Hain, showed that the store opened June 21, 1849 and dissolved July 24, 1850. Dr. Hain, a great-grandson of Spalding, gave the day book to Western Michigan University.

Anyone who has lived in Dowagiac the past 10 years has seen this building for it stood on Commercial Street and housed the Dowagiac Pastry Shop and the John Scott Insurance Agency for many years.

After 1850 the building was moved, as buildings often were in the early days, and was occupied by the old Alhambra saloon. It was Dowagiac's Post Office during the Civil War.

But it housed bakeries most of its existence, the old Preuss Bakery, then the Solf Bakery for at least 50 years, a restaurant and finally the Dowagiac Pastry Shop.

Of all the stores that were here in the early days, this seems to be the only book preserved although it only covered 13 months.

The items people bought sound pretty fascinating at times. Local druggists and doctors will shudder at this. Thornton Lowman bought a half ounce of opium along with a "hand saw, hammer, 8 yards of drb. delaine, $2.00; 1 yd. cambric and 4 yds. fringe, 45 cents; hands. and silk and spool cot. 19 cents." Dr. Brayton bought ½ dr. morphine for 44 cents; also a padlock for 19 cents and a broom, 19 cents.

People bought a great variety of things, including books, shoes, castor oil, epsom salts, potatoes, mouse traps, lamp oil, playing cards, candlesticks, whalebones, tea, coffee, fish hooks, Isaac Shurte bought a set of Canton blue dishes for $20.78.

And whortleberries, vest chains, molasses, sauce plates, cheese, barrel of mackerel, table linen, camphor, door handles, pills, yarn, red flannel, kid gloves, almanac and much, much more.

What a marvelous flea market it would make today.

10

A Spaulding Letter

Through the kindess of the late Dr. Harold Spalding Hain and his wife, Sylvia, I was given a copy of a letter written by Erastus Holmes Spalding in 1853.

In Dowagiac's early days many local residents sent their chidlren back east to be educated, particularly their sons, and who usually lived with relatives. The letter was believed written to his son, Lyman Barker Spalding, and who probably was attending school in western New York. The Spaldings came from around Lockport.

Erastus Holmes Spalding came to Cass County in 1833 from Scipio, New York, where he was born in 1801. He was the great-grandfather of Dr. Hain. His son, Lyman, married Mary Renesten, daughter of William Renesten, who built a carding mill just outside Dowagiac in 1830 and a grist mill in 1833. It was William Renesten who dammed up the Dowagiac Creek, resulting in the present Dowagiac Millpond. He sold his grist mill to Erastus Holmes Spalding in 1834 and moved to his farm in LaGrange Township.

Dowagiac did not have a high school in 1853, only an elementary school since 1840, sometimes public, sometimes private, so Lyman and his younger brother, Erastus were sent east to school.

Erastus Holmes Spalding was a well educated man for his times, a shrewd businessman and had a hand in many affairs before he died in 1869.

Spalding Street (or Spaulding as it is now spelled) was named for him. He built a store here and owned three different mills in Dowagic and Lake LaGrange or Whitmanville as it was called. His letter, dated Mary 14, 1853, Dowagiac, is as follows:

Mr Dear Son:

Your favour of the 6th came duly to hand and was perused with pleasure. I will endeavor to answer your many inquiries. In the first place I am much gratified to see that you are anxious about your school and have a disposition to profit by it, but going to school only a part of the year gives you a start in the branches of useful education. To make it fully answer the end intended it is necessary to use all the leisure hours you have in reviewing the studies you have begun to bring them to practical use, what you learn at school is of no use further than to give a start, using the leisure moments as they present, is just as necessary to finish up that which is begun at school as the going to school is to get the start. But in no case slight your work or neglect to gain time, do everything well which you undertake, a half finished job is no credit to the doer. Finish what you undertake, do nothing halfway.

I hope you will progress in phonography, there is no knowing where the chances of life may throw us, or what may be most usefull, but one thing is certain we cannot know too much if we only make a good use of it.

Mr. Carlisle is helping me tend the old mill. I almost fear it will fall down when the frost comes out of the ground. The Whitmanville mill was burnt about the 1st of this month with the large yellow building that stood near it. This adds considerably to our grinding. We have about all we can do now in the way of grinding. I hope it will not fall down before another mill can be built.

The town has not grown on our side the railroad because the mill was destroyed but as soon as there is one started this side must grow. I sold out the store before I was east the last time.

There is five drygoods stores, 4 groceries, 2 drug stores, and 2 taverns, 2 shoe shops and one shoe store, 1 pin shop, 1 cabinet shop, 2 blacksmith shops, 2 shops where they make sash doors and (?) and there is 1 Baptist Church and the Methdodists talk of putting up one this summer. The town generally is improving.

One store, Lybrook, Lofland and Sons have bought this season, 1,003 hogs for which they have paid $11,675.00, besides the wheat and corn and oats, they sold their stock of drygoods out so close they have had to replenish from Detroit and are now fixing to start for the city.

Through the winter there has been frequently from 100 to 150 teams at a time in town and I don't see anything to hinder Dowagiac from being quite a town. We have had a very open winter here but March comes in rather rough, it has been colder since March came in that it was in February.

There has been no letters received from your Uncle Frank or Howard since Jan. 1852. Why they don't write I can't see. There is a man that went from Berrien last year that is in with them by the name of Armstrong who writes to his family occasionally and in that way Aunt Eliza hears from them. Uncle Frank is expected here in June next, it is said they are doing well but they aren't very strong. I have written about eight letters to them and have heard nothing and give it up.

Aunt Eliza is not going to California. She has got her lot fenced and plowed and means to stay in Berrien. Elizabeth is married to John D. Barber, August and Nett is with their mother. They have all been sick this winter and Aunt was very sick but they are well wno. I was there last week. I saw Frank at Berrien last spring, and is the only time I have seen him since I saw you. I heard from him a few days since, he was well and going to school. I will do(e) your errand when I see him.

I am greatly disappointed in us visiting you the past winter and shall come and see you as soon after navigation opens as I can. Erie is very well and talks a great deal about you and Erastus, amost every day he asks when we are going to see you.

I should be glad to see a good mill built at Dowagiac how as the mill is gone at Whitmanville. It would be quite an advantage to have those mills out of the way.

There are a great many going from these parts to California this spring. Frank Spalding, 3 of the Andrews, in all some 8 from Dowagiac, and Berrien is to take quite a poke also among them Geo. Essick. I think there is more going this time than there were last spring -- but I cannot get ready.

I am glad to hear of the general good health of all of our friends. Hoping soon to see you, when I hope to hear a good account of you both. At present I don't know what I shall do but I think there will be a chance for one to do something after awhile. My greatest anxiety is for my children, but if they do as they ought or as well as they know they will be well cared for, or your main study be to do right, be cautious about telling tales as a close mouth denotes a wise head, but never vary from the truth, be dutiful and kind to all and be obedient to your seniors. Set Erastus a good example and encourage him in doing well and trying to learn his books. I shall expect to see you much improved as you ought to be from the chance you have had.

Remember me affectionately to your uncle and Aunt Webster and to your Aunt Jane and say to her she is often thought of by me. Give my love to Samuel and Wife and say to them for me to make Erastus mind -- I hope he will do well from choice, as everybody feels best when they do what is right. I will try to see you soon. Remember me to all that enquire.

Truly Your Father,
E.H. Spalding

11

The Wigwam

By the 1860's most of the people in the Dowagiac area were intensely Republican. I had run across mention of the Wigwam that stood on Commercial Street, and finally came up with its history probably written by Abner Moon.

The "great wigwam" was erected during Abraham Lincoln's first presidential campaign, "a building which at that time had no equal for size in southern Michigan. Politics were at a white heat in those days.

"Every Republican in this part of the country became interested in the building of this wigwam, and the farmers also took a hand in it.

"A frame was put up, with posts 10 feet apart, and the sides of the building consisted of rails nailed to these posts and furnished by the farmers. A good roof completed the structure.

"It stood on Commercial Street, one end facing New York Avenue and the other the alley, and occupied the ground now occupied by the library building. It was 100 feet long by 50 wide, and there was standing room in it for 1,500 people.

"Such men as Zach Chandler, Ben Wade, J.C. Burrows, Senator Howard and other orators of nation wide fame spoke in this wigwam. All during the campaign of 1860 there was something doing there every week or two.

"The rallies were something remarkable. A team of 40 yoke of cattle was furnished by farmers, some as far away as Keeler Township, and at the shops of P.D. Beckwith a platform was made for trucks. It held several men all splitting rails during the parades.

This platform was 14 feet wide and 20 feet long, and when the long team of oxen passed by, the rail splitters always got the best of the cheering.

"The building had a side entrance on Commercial Street, and sat back from the street a few feet. It remained there until the next year, before it was torn down. It did its part toward electing Mr. Lincoln, for which very few were sorry at the time."

12

Newspapers

The late Harry H. Whiteley, publisher of the Dowagiac Daily News for 40 years, compiled a history of Cass County newspapers. He was born in Gladwin and published several weeklies in northern Michigan before coming to Dowagiac in 1916 to take over the management of The Daily News. He was also a nationally-known conservationist and one of the founders of the Michigan Conservation Department.

"Newspaper history began in Dowagiac in 1850 and after more than half a century of vigorous journalism in which papers rose and fell, consolidations began which resulted in the survival of The Dowagiac Daily News as the sole newspaper of this city since May 4, 1912.

"Following the destruction of the plant of the Cass County Times and the Cass County Republican in 1854, James L. Gantt established The Cass County Tribune in the same year, June 5, 1854. In 1858 his policy became 'distasteful' to the Republican leaders, it is recorded, and failing in efforts to buy him out, they induced W.H. Campbell and H.B. Jones to establish the Republican as a rival. In 1859 Mr. Gantt succumbed to the Republican which continued for 22 years as the sole newspaper of the community. The committee which was responsible for the establishment ·of The Republican was Justus Gage, Jesse G. Beeson, Walter G. Beckwith, Joshua Lofland and William Sprague.

Other owners included Charles A. Smith, Jesse G. Roe, H.C. Buffington, Richard Holmes and C.J. Greenleaf, said Whiteley. When R.N. Kellogg bought the plant in 1880, he changed the name to Dowagiac Republican. He was followed by E.H. Spoor, Becraft & Amsden, Becraft & Son and J.O. Becraft alone, who retained ownership until 1904 when he sold to H.E. Agnew. He made it into a semi-weekly for four years when in 1909 it went back to its weekly form.

Its first competition came in 1880 when W.M. Wooster moved his Lawrence Advertiser from Van Buren County and named it The Dowagiac Times. Abner M. Moon, who was editing The Marcellus News and bought The Times, selling it to James Heddon in 1885 who published it for many years. It joined the general merger in 1912.

A couple of daily newspapers were published, and only for very brief periods. A third weekly in Dowagiac was The Standard published from 1892 to 1897, first by J.N. Klock, then R.E. Curtis, and J.A. Webster, who sold it to Abner Moon and who changed its name to The Herald.

On February 6, 1897 was published the first issue of The Dowagiac Daily News by 20-year old Charles Heddon, and issued from The Times office.

Shortly before this there was published the Tri-Weekly Monitor, but it was not long-lived.

Whiteley said, "The pressure of the inevitable can be seen as now the field was over-filled with The Daily News, The Times, The Herald and The Republican -- one daily, two weeklies, and one semi-weekly." The Republican and Herald were consolidated in 1909 and began to issue a daily paper in opposition to The Daily News and known as The Daily Herald. The Daily News and Times had already consolidated.

In the next three years all kinds of changes took place among the weeklies, Abner Moon bought out Agnew; The Dowagiac Publishing Company (Daily News) absorbed The Herald and the Weekly Republican-Herald. The latter continued briefly as "Moon's Weekly," and by the end of the year it succumbed and Moon joined The Daily News staff. This left The Dowagiac Daily News alone in the field.

13

The First Telephone

Very few people are alive today who can remember when the first telephone came to Dowagiac, or who will remember that the Dowagiac system developed a "first" in the state as is related in a history written by Robert Bolduc when he was manager of the General Telephone Company here a few years ago. Only older people will remember the old Home telephone, a big, ponderous nickel-plated "dial" telephone.

It was during the year 1890 that the first telephone was installed in Dowagiac. This connection with the outside world was established over a grounded line between Kalamazoo and Niles, and had its headquarters in a furniture store owned by Charles Bigelow on the corner of Pennsylvania Avenue and Commercial Street, where the Post Office building is now located.

Later this telephone was moved into the drug store of R. Lewis on Front Street. In 1894, this long distance line, which was still a grounded one, was still housed in the drug store. Structurally it consisted of a small jack box made up of three jacks with a toll line connected to one of them and two other wires running out from each of the others in opposite directions from the store.

Because they were grounded circuits, these wires had a number of private telephones looped in. These were located in the Lee Bank, Frank Lyle's residence, Fred E. Lee's residence, the Drill Works and the Elkerton Hotel. Another line led to the Round Oak offices and several other residences. Practically all of the operating was done by the late Arthur Rudolphi who was then clerking in Lewis's drug store.

In 1895 and 1896, the Bell company, which was at the time the only company operating in the state, built an entirely new exchange here, setting poles wherever needed and establishing a central office and switchboard in the rear of the drug store.

The construction work was in charge of a foreman named William McCue, and it was the first all metallic circuit exchange built in Michigan. The switchboard was known as the No. 3 type magneto, consisting of one position with an ultimate equipment of 75 lines. There were 60 telephones connected with the new exchange. Arthur Rudolphi was still head drug clerk and chief operator and Sidney Mosher was his assistant and dispenser of soda water.

Emmet Platt, who several years later was manager of the Dowagiac Telephone Company, was working here during the time of this early installation. It was he who connected the switchboard and installed the first telephones throughout the city, later supervising repair work and making additions while working out of Kalamazoo. At this time the Dowagiac Telephone Exchange was looked upon as a model type and was often referred to throughout the state as such.

Then in 1897, the first local company was organized under the management of Will Heddon and Dan White, known as the Heddon Telephone Company. Here was the Bell Company's first competitor. An exchange was built above a store located on what is now the Redner grocery property. (Later Hart Jewelry Store and recently torn down.) The rates were twelve and eighteen dollars a year as against the Bell's thirty-six dollars per year for residence service and forty-eight dollars for commercial.

Mr. Heddon stated: "We commenced operation with about 150 telephones and 200 capacity switchboard. Through the generosity of Mr. Lee, for whom I was working as an electrician on salary, in allowing me to devote the time necessary to manage the exchange, it was only necessary to employ one trouble shooter and two operators, and we prospered far beyond our expectations. About two years from the building of the exchange I took a position as manager of the Central Telephone Company in Kalamazoo of which Mr. Lee was a stockholder, and soon Mr. Lee, 'Uncle Dan' and myself pooled our interests and sold to the Bell Company."

On account of local interests, Heddon's little company secured the majority of the business, and soon had built long distance lines between Dowagiac, Niles and Kalamazoo.

In 1900, the Michigan Telephone Company, which was a part of the Erie Telephone System, connected with the Bell as a sublicensed company, purchased and combined the properties of the Central and Heddon companies and established an office in the Vrooman building. The construction was all rebuilt with a very expensive type of equipment for those days. It was then that the hundreds of large Idaho cedar poles were set on Front, Main, Orchard, Green and Commercial Streets, and a large amount of cable installed.

In 1907 a new company was organized and prompted to operate an independent system in Cass County. It was called the Cass County Home Telephone Company. Automatic service was installed, thus making it a serious competitor of the Bell Company. For a period of years this new organization did a thriving, but not a profitable business, and eventually began to lose customers to the Bell Company. Competition was so keen that neither company made money, with the result that the Cass County Company went into bankruptcy about the year 1919. For several years it operated under a receivership with George Hall, the former manager, as receiver, and was finally sold at a receiver's sale to George Phillips.

(Older people will remember that business houses and professional people were forced to have both the Home and Bell telephones installed for the convenience of their customers. Some would have the Home system and others the Bell.)

On May 1, 1923, the Dowagiac Telephone Company was formed to take over the property of the Cass County Home and the Bell Telephone companies' interests. The plants were consolidated in September and housed in the central office of the Bell Company. The old automatic equipment was displaced and the offices abandoned.

In 1924 a small amount of underground conduit was laid and the outside construction rearranged in order to remove the poles in the business section. This particular work also eliminated many poles throughout the residence district—about 300 in all. The work was not completed until 1925.

In the spring of 1926 the Van Buren County Telephone Company purchased the controlling interest of the Dowagiac Telephone Company, continuing its operations under the old name until the formation and consolidation of various other properties into the Tri-County Telephone Company, which has been responsible for elevating the local branch to its present status.

Tri-County became Union Telephone Company in 1949. It became General Telephone in 1957.

by Robert Bolduc

14

The Automobile

, Dowagiac never turned out to be a second Detroit—but it was not because some of its citizens didn't try. Two automobile companies were born in 1908, the Lindsley Company and the Dowagiac Motor Car Company. The Lindsley Company, which was first, actually began as the Dowagiac Automobile Company. The factory was started by Frank Lake and D.L. "Dode" Neff in the Farr Sand Band building on East Railroad Street at LaGrange Street, with the office in front.

Victor Lindsley bought them out on June 3, 1908. Two men, Dee Carney of this city and Albert McIntosh of Buchanan worked in the shop part, with Frank Lake as the manager. Lindsley, after his arrival from Chicago, moved the offices upstairs over what is now the Underwood Shoe Store on the corner of Front and Commerical Streets. Georgia Penrod, who died in 1975, was the bookkeeper and entire office force. She said that Lindsley had ideas too large for his small budget and the company went bankrupt on Dec. 5, 1908.

Frank Lake, Leon Lyle and Malcolm Campbell, who had started the Dowagiac Automobile Company, took over the Lindsley assets, paying $4,500. There were 15 cars on hand.

There are two Lindsley cars which have been restored in existence today. One is in Florida and the other in Auburn, Illinois.

A description of the Lindsley car was found in a catalog called Floyd Clymer's Historical Motor Scrapbook published in 1943, and which reprinted the following ad:

49

$250 makes you a 12 horse power auto with the Lindsley Car chassis. The Lindsley Car is the best high wheel auto ever produced. We furnish all the parts for making your wagon or buggy into a buggy automobile for only $250.

"Bear in mind that this is exactly the same engine and parts used in the celebrated Model B Lindsley Car. Remember—this includes every part required to make a complete job. Engine and transmission connected to run. Every part guaranteed.

"Everyone may now own an automobile. No credit, no discounts, no agents. The goods worth more money. If you mean business write at once to the J.V. Lindsley Auto Chassis Co., Dowagiac, Mich."

Victor Lindsley may have failed to become an automobile tycoon, but he was one of several Lindsley brothers, who took the old Lindsley Lumber Company, founded by their father, John Lindsley in the 1880's, from Dowagiac to Florida and established a chain of lumber yards—a multi-million dollar business.

Victor Lindsley and his wife were killed in an automobile accident in Florida in the 1960's as they were en route to attend a Dowagiac-Florida reunion.

The Dowagiac Motor Car

The Dowagiac Motor Car Company was organized in 1908 and was a going concern by 1909. It was begun by Frank Lake and D.L. Neff, with Leon Lyle joining the company a little later. Neff later established the first automobile garage in Dowagiac. This company might have continued much longer had not two of its executives, Frank Lake and Leon Lyle been killed in an accident.

Other stockholders in this company were Malcolm A. Campbell, Clark S. Finch, Willis M. Farr, John Kauffman and Fred Dunnington.

On April 13, 1909 the company was doing so well that three of its vehicles were shipped to Argentina.

The Dowagiac Daily News on Feb. 17, 1909 published a story and a picture of the motor delivery wagon which stated: "This is an auto truck wagon and is the largest of three sizes which the company will make—the three having carrying capacities of 1,000 pounds, 1,500 pounds and 2,000 pounds. It is driven by a couple of 34 horse power engines.

The car is built like a touring car and is therefore in a class by itself. Some of the strong points are here mentioned. A magneto is used. The frames are all hot riveted. The jack shaft runs in two 8-inch and two 4-inch Hayett flexible rollers, and is housed in crucible steel the full length.

"The wheel bearings are of the celebrated Weston-Mott make. The wheels are 36 inches in diameter, and carry 3-inch solid rubber tires both front and rear. For axles heavy eyebeams are used and the planatary transmission is made to their own design. It has detachable side-sprockets and the body is 6 feet 6 inches in length by 41 inches wide in rear of the seat, having 9-inch panels and 8-inch wings.

"This car was exhibited at the Chicago Auto Show last week where it attracted a great deal of interest. Several sales resulted on the spot.

"It was driven to Dowagiac from Chicago by Frank Lake and Leon Lyle. Leaving Chicago at 4 p.m. they drove to Hobart, Ind. 40 miles distant, and stayed overnight. They left the next morning at 7:30, driving through several cities including Michigan City, South Bend and Niles, through mud and snow and drifts four feet deep in places, and arrived home in the evening, the truck making the trip without problems.

"The first car was sold to a Mr. Lockwood of Washington, D.C. and shipped there to him."

Just how many others were sold is not known and if there is a Dowagiac motor delivery wagon in existence, no one has heard of it.

Frank Lake and Leon Lyle were killed June 20, 1909 en route home from Chicago, ironically enough, not in an automobile but in a street car accident near Chesterton, Ind.

Frank Lake was said to be the inventive genius of the company and Leon Lyle the capable manager. The company was sold to a Tulsa, Oklahoma firm and soon died there.

Dowagiac's first automobile

The first automobile ever driven in Dowagiac arrived in this city on August 1, 1899. It was a Haynes-Apperson and was owned by Archie Gardner. It was considered of such importance at the time that spectators came for miles to look at the machine. In an account of its arrival published in The Daily News, the word "automobile" was capitalized every time it was mentioned.

"An Automobile, the first of the horseless carriage family to be seen on the streets of Dowagiac, was purchased recently by A.B. Gardner and arrived in this city last evening from Kokomo, Ind. On account of its novelty as a pioneer in the locomotion line, it is at present interesting our citizens.

"The carriage is a large affair, weighing about 6,500 pounds and its motive power is produced by a gasoline engine of about seven horsepower. Its wheels are pneumatic tired, it is supplied with two seats and when on a good road can carry a load of passengers at a speed of 15 to 20 miles an hour.

"The Automobile was manufactured in Kokomo and is designed for pleasure riding alone. It will be operated in and about the city by Mr. Gardner." The car was driven here from Kokomo the trip taking five days. "Mr. Gardner went down to ride back with the machine but got tired of the trip and came on ahead on a train."

The Daily News also reported that on the night the automobile arrived in the city, "a party of local Masons journeyed to Pokagon to give the third degree to Russ Cook, the Pokagon man who was killed at a crossing accident at that village that winter. On the road between here and Pokagon, the Masons encountered the new Automobile." Many of them had never seen a car before and the horses they were driving did everyting but climb the fences.

None of the party could imagine what was coming, as they could hear the car long before they could see it. One of the survivors of that occasion in later years reported that would always remember first hearing the machine coming and described the noise as the racket "that might be expected if bundles of barbed wire were bounded continuously from the roof of the Beckwith building to the pavement."

The late Don Moon remembered that this car was somewhat temperamental and that on frequent occasions it would have to be hauled back to the Gardner home by a team of horses. In fact, Gardner often times used to tell his man just what road he was going to take for his trip. Then after the automobile had started out, the man would hitch up the team and drive off after him. It was only on rare occasions that he missed the opportunity to haul the car home.

15

Beckwith Theater

The Beckwith Memorial Theater, which was opened and dedicated in January, 1893 in the newly constructed Beckwith building on Front Street, was built as a memorial to Philo D. Beckwith. At that time it was the second memorial theater in the world and the first to honor an American citizen.

Beckwith was a lover of the theater and the arts and a generous patron of many theatrical ventures, concerts and lectures here. When he died in 1889 members of his family thought that a memorial theater would be a fitting tribute to this man.

Dowagiac was home to a number of theatrical people and this was a community appreciative of this venture.

No expense was spared in its construction, and lengthy descriptions of the building and of the theater it contained were carried in Chicago newspapers. One called it "the finest little playhouse in America, a perfect little gem; the only fault we have to find with it, it isn't in Chicago."

The building was constructed of Lake Superior red sandstone, a strip of which is still visible on the wall that bordered it. It was a unique building for the busts that were carved on its facade. Noted women included George Eliot, George Sand, Mary Anderson, Sarah Bernhardt, Rachel and Susan B. Anthony.

Directly over the main entrance was the portrait of P.D. Beckwith. Other portrait medallions were of Beethoven, Chopin, Rossini, Wagner, Verdi, Liszt, Voltaire, Ingersoll, Thomas Paine, Victor Hugo, Ralph Waldo Emerson, Walt Whitman, Goethe and the immortal Shakespeare.

When the building was demolished in the 1960's, nearly all of the medallions were preserved and are in the safekeeping of Southwestern Michigan College near Dowagiac. Several have been installed in the entrance pillars at the college.

There were 15 dressing rooms in the theater; luxurious boxes with silken hangings; overstuffed high pile mohair plush seats, dyed n light fawn and flesh colors. The plush for the seats was sent to Germany to be dyed to harmonize with the decorations on the walls and ceilings.

Besides the main floor there was a balcony and above that "the peanut gallery," and usually filled with young people.

On the opening night, January 20, 1893 everyone was in full evening dress and diamonds and other jewels sparkled all over the theater. The audience was a distinguished one with theater parties from Chicago, Detroit, Kalamazoo, Grand Rapids, as well as other places.

An old tattered clipping I have lists many of the women present with a description of their dresses. Mlle. Rhea the French actress, the leading women for the two nights her company was there, wore a double strand of diamonds.

The opening play was Shakespeare's "Much Ado About Nothing." Mlle. Rhea's leading man was William S. Hart, better known in later years as the hero of many a western cowboy movie. On the second' night her company presented "Josephine," an historical play with William S. Hart as Napoleon. The theater was formally dedicated on January 25, 1893 with Col. Robert Ingersoll speaking on "Shakespeare."

The Beckwith Memorial Theater Orchestra, directed by Arthur E. Rudolphi, acquitted itself with brilliance. This orchestra was an integral part of the theater, but it also played for many other events in the community. Archie Gardner, grandson of P.D. Beckwith, was the first manager of the theater.

The programs for the first three nights were given to me and I still have them together with a few others from 1903, these being ordinary printed ones. The first three are printed on satin ribbon and enclosed in folders.

Some of the country's greatest stage stars played in this theater and often Dowagiac was one of a couple stops between Detroit and Chicago. Theater lovers from all over the area came to this playhouse.

It is impossible to name all who played there, Helene Modjeska, the famous Polish actress; Thomas W. Keene, America's noted tragedian, appeared here in "Richard III"; Julia Marlowe in "The Hunchback"; Roland Reed in "The Politician"; Walker Whiteside in "Hamlet". Frederick Power of Dowagiac was a member of this company for a time.

Many of these stage stars were entertained in the homes of local residents and often gave readings at local clubs.

Daniel Frohman's company presented "The Prisoner of Zenda"; Otis Skinner starred in "Rosemary". A brilliant performance was given by Robert Mantell in "The Dagger and the Cross", in September 1899. Sarah Bernhardt was scheduled to come but her performance had to be cancelled due to her illness.

When Richard Mansfield's Garrick Theater company played at the Beckwith in "Trilby", a special train was run to Dowagiac, for Detroit, Grand Rapids and Dowagiac were the only cities in Michigan to be visited.

The Gilbert Comic Opera Company delighted everyone. And there was Lewis Morrison in "Faust", and Murray and Mack in "Finnegan's Ball". "Madame X", "The Woman in Black", "Dr. Jekyll and Mr. Hyde", they were all seen here.

The Beckwith Theater had many changes of scenery and was very modern for its day.

Rose Coghlan came in "The Greatest Thing in the World," and the original cast of Denman Thompson's "The Old Homestead", as well as many good stock companies. They presented such well known tear jerkers as "Uncle Tom's Cabin", "Way Down East", "East Lynn", and others. Rose Melville, who used to summer at Diamond Lake near Cassopolis, played in her famous role of "Sis Hopkins", more than once.

And John Philip Sousa usually put on two performances as well as a parade, preceding the matinee.

Fisk O'Hara, Jack Norworth and Nora Bayes, and even the Four

Marx Brothers, we had them all.

The late George Chapman recalled that the famous old play, "Charley's Aunt," and still revived from time to time, first saw the light of day on the stage of the Beckwith Theater. Only then it was called "Playing on the Dog."

The cast members were all professionals who came from Dowagiac. It included the comedian, George Ober, whose wife, Ada Clarke Murray, was a well known actress, Fred Powers, Hattie Clarke Sprague, Bert Sprague and Stella Mayhew who was a Clarke. The old Joseph Clarke home still stands at 206 Green Street. The only amateur was Katy Merwin of Dowagiac. They took the play to the Power Opera House in Chicago where it was a flop.

Katy Merwin afterwards married Cecil Harris who had come here to work in the Round Oak offices. Cecil's brother, Paul Harris, used to come from Chicago to spend his weekends, and later was founder of Rotary International. In fact he was working on the idea while staying at the Round Oak cottage at Sister Lakes.

The Beckwith Teater served the community well. Our high school commencement programs were held there as well as our school plays and many other events. The walls of the lobby were lined with autographed photographs of the many actors and actresses who had played there and many have wondered what became of this valuable collection.

The three-story building also housed the Dowagiac Post office; Lee Brothers Bank; the Round Oak offices and the City Council Chambers.

Stage plays became scarce as motion pictures began taking over the field, and the Beckwith Theater was finally converted into a movie.

In time the building was sold to an out of town resident who cared nothing for the town or tradition. If it had happened a few years later when historic preservation became more common, it is possible that local residents, who were shocked at the building's destruction, could have instituted a "Save the Beckwith" movement.

16

The Early Years

Richard Holmes, who was editing the old Dowagiac Republican, wrote the story of the Round Oak Company while its founder was still alive. Quoting from a story Holmes wrote for a July 1885 issue, he said:

"Thirty years ago P.D. Beckwith came to Dowagiac full of life and energy and lots of days of hard work. This city was then about 10 years old, the streets were one continuous bed of loose sand. Only one church (Baptist) and a small one story school house comprised the extend of our public buildings.

"Time passed and five churches have been built, a two-story school house, since burned down, and replaced by our now large commodious and beautiful Union building (old Central School) and a no less beautiful Ward building (site of present Justus Gage School), both of them now surrounded by groves of ornamental and shade trees, with grass plats in abundance for the pleasure of all and especially our children."

"The amount of Mr. Beckwith's business consisted at first of a two horse power steam engine, and one workman and himself making about 500 lbs. castings per week, while now about 7 tons of stove castings were turned out every day."

Holmes went on to say that "the printing for the business has reached such magnitude that it was found necessary to add a printing department. The old office building has been moved to a convenient place, an addition built to it, where steam power is supplied from the main engine and in which is now running a steam power printing press, entirely upon work for the Round Oak Stove Works.

This is now The Dowagiac Commercial Press.

Holmes also wrote that "14 years ago our townsman, Mr. O.G. Beach was employed as traveling agent to introduce the stove to the public, traveling only in Michigan. There were about 300 stoves sold the first year and the number was then thought to be a great success."

The following year Holmes wrote another story for the Republican about the Round Oak: "A new 20-ton cupola, requiring seven tons of boiler and cast iron, four carloads of common brick and two carloads of fire brick in its construction, has been erected and supplied with a steam elevator for hoisting coal and iron to the cupola, by means of which one man can do the work of several in the old days."

He described other improvements including "this new workshop is certainly a pleasant, light and airy department and is in full view of the main street of our city, the railroad depot and much of the surrounding country adjacent to the city and the works.

"The Michigan Central Railroad Company has built a side track to the yard of the new building, whereby iron and coal can be unloaded in the yard only a few feet from the door of the elevator, which is a great convenience to the workmen.

"A fireproof vault has been constructed for the safety of the hundreds of patterns which are more valuable than the buildings of the entire property. New sand and coal sheds have been built and moulding sand is now being shipped from Albany, N.Y. for use in the foundry." And this was almost a century ago.

I should add that in time the Round Oak acquired a sales force that covered the entire country. All came back to Dowagiac to meet together at least once a year, sometimes here for 10 days to two weeks.

17

The Round Oak

Unless some one is a native of Dowagiac or the area -- they do not realize the important part the Round Oak Company played in the development and history of Dowagiac. It was the genius of Philo D. Beckwith or "P.D." as he was called by his workmen, that contributed so much to the growth and progress of this community. All one has to do is to go over old newspapers which recorded the progress of the company in almost every issue.

In the beginning stove-making and the manufacture of the roller grain drill were combined. But it was P.D. Beckwith's invention of the underdraft stove which made this an industrial community.

In about the year 1850 a man named Davis started a machine shop here, only two years after the arrival of the railroad. It was located on what is now Park Place west of the railroad. Beckwith, who came to Michigan, to Battle Creek, and Niles, arrived in Dowagiac in 1854 and bought out Davis. A year or two later he bought an acre of ground from Justus Gage on South Front Street on the Dowagiac Creek and moved his shop and foundry there. It was here that he started the manufacture of the roller grain drill invented by John S. Gage.

It was while at this location that Beckwith made a stove to heat his shop. How Michigan Central officials heard of it, no one has said, but they asked him to make one for the Dowagiac depot. It did such a good job that he was asked to make other stoves for other depots along the line.

He was becoming crowded where he was and in 1868 he bought

two acres across the railroad tracks near the depot. This was the nucleus of what was to become one of the largest manufacturers in the world of heating stoves. He began a regular business of manufacturing stoves in 1872 and his stove was patented in 1873.

He had rough going in his early days here, and a great-grandson, the late Jack Gardner, said that Beckwith was often obliged to go to local merchants to borrow money with which to meet the weekly payroll.

But Beckwith made a good product and there was a great demand for it. He constantly expanded the factory, and had the foresight to see the importance of the stove business. He added improvements continually, and in 1886 the first Round Oak furnace was manufactured. Later the Round Oak range was added, and for years the name Round Oak was carried around the world.

In 1879 Fred E. Lee joined the company, having married Kate Beckwith in 1878. He worked in the office and then traveled on the road. Five years before P.D. Beckwith died, in 1889, he was called back to take charge of the office. He carried forward the very successful business started by his father-in-law.

No other stove could compete in quality with the Round Oak as is evidenced by the many still in existence today and cherished as collectors' items. People write to Dowagiac from coast to coast, and from Canada wanting to know more about the history of this marvelous stove they just bought, and where can they find repair parts for it. A Round Oak range which probably cost less than $100 when new, was recently advertised for $2,000.

Very scarce today is the Round Oak baseburner -- a handsome big heating stove, all nickel plated, with a square of ising glass windows set in each side. The only fuel that can be used in this stove is chestnut hard coal. We had one in our living room and my mother or grandmother would pop popcorn and with a pan of good Michigan apples we sat around the stove on a cold winter's night. They often turned out the lights, the glow and little blue flames shining through the windows were light enough. Who needed anything more?

Through the years the company had many souvenirs made, plates, steins, spoons, calendars, pictures, mostly showing the famous Round Oak Indian. These are collectors' items too.

Quality may have been one of the reasons for the gradual downfall of the Round Oak Company, and too high an overhead in order to compete with other manufacturers, along with various changes in ownership during its last years.

World War II caused the factory to be sold to the Kaiser-Fraser Company and no more stoves, ranges or furnaces were manufactured after that time. However Round Oak water heaters were made along with some other products until recent years. The Peerless Company of Indianapolis bought the company, and it in turn was swallowed up by a larger firm, not connected with stove or furnace manufacturing and it too "bit the dust."

In its hey day close to 1,500 men were employed by the Round Oak -- and for years almost everyone in Dowagiac had some working connection with the company. Several generations worked there and took great pride in it. Local people are still very sentimental about the Round Oak. Quite a few own Round Oak stoves they just keep because they do not want to part with them. Many homes are still heated by the long-lasting Round Oak furnaces, testifying to their excellent construction.

The Round Oak always had exhibits at many state fairs. Featured was the famous gold-plated Round Oak stove, now owned by Southwestern Michigan College near Dowagiac. The college also owns Kate Beckwith Lee's own stove covered with iron "lace" with her name on the stove. The college also has quite a collection of Round Oak mementoes.

The complex of Round Oak buildings is still here and put to good use by the Jessco Company. The oldest ones are over 80 years old and giving good service today, much to the satisfaction of Round Oak old timers.

It was a great wrench to the citizens of this community when the Beckwith building was razed -- another link broken that connected the community with this once great industry.

There were other furnace companies here, all "spin offs" from the Round Oak -- the Rudy, Premier and Steel Furnace Company -- they are all gone. Dowagiac once known as the "Furnace City of America," doesn't manufacture a single furnace or stove today.

Other companies making different products occupy these factories today.

18

The Round Oak Range

In writing about Round Oak stoves, it must be remembered that the Round Oak range, some of which were made to handle gas, wood or coal, was a highly valued member of the Round Oak family. The following story which appeared in the Dowagiac Daily News on October 18, 1911, gives some idea of the extent to which Round Oak products traveled.

"Captain Otto Sverdrup, who piloted the Scandinavian ship, 'Fram' in which Nansen made his celebrated trips in the hope of reaching the North Pole, is to become the possessor of a Round Oak Chief steel range.

"Through the Minneapolis agency of the Beckwith Estate his order for one of the famous Dowagiac ranges was entered a few days ago. It has just reached the offices in this city, and shipment is now being prepared to reach New York City in time for a steamship on the Scandinavian-American line leaving New York on October 26th.

"Its destination is to be Christiana, Norway, the home of the celebrated captain. It was the purchaser's instructions that the range should be equipped with a 30-gallon range boiler and stand.

"Captain Sverdrup has just been in Minneapolis on a visit, and while there he saw demonstrated one of the Round Oak Chief steel ranges. So high pleased with it was he that he at once entered his order for one.

"Providing the range shipped him proves as satisfactory and successful as those he saw in operation in Minneapolis it means that a dozen or fifteen more will be purchased forthwith by people at

Christiana.

"When Friedhof Nansen equipped his famous ship 'Fram' to make a dash for the North Pole he commissioned Captain Sverdrup to pilot the ship. On each of the Nansen expeditions Captain Sverdrup was its captain. He stands high among the Scandinavian people, and while in Minneapolis was very much lionized. He has relatives there, but his recent visit widened his acquaintance into extensive proportions.

"Round Oak stoves and ranges are used in every country on the civilized globe, but it remains for the famous Norwegian captain to introduce them in Christiana, the Norwegian capital."

As a child we lived for a time in Seattle, Wash. and one Sunday afternoon, the family took a walk down to the waterfront. There in a big warehouse, we saw, in looking through the windows, dozens of Round Oak stoves, probably going to the Orient.

19

The Round Oak Whistle

The Round Oak whistle -- how many in the community remember its deep-throated bass "voice" as it floated -- not only over the city and countryside but could be heard in four counties in Michigan and sometimes in Indiana.

This of course was in the days when motorized traffic was scarce and when the winds were right, sounds could be carried for miles.

People in the community set their clocks by the Round Oak whistle -- they lived by it as did farmers and others all over the area. Everybody knew what time it was.

Its powerful bellow was not unpleasant, a deep bass sound that carried for miles. Decatur, Marcellus, Cassopolis, Vandalia, Edwardsburg, Berrien Springs, Berrien Center, and even Niles could hear it as they have testified in days past.

As a small child we lived on a farm a few miles outside Vandalia and when the sun was low in the sky, the Round Oak whistle would sound off, and to me it was the sun thundering.

It gave off two blasts at quarter of seven in the morning and the workman knew he must be on his way. It blew once at 7 a.m., and at 12 noon. Workmen had an hour off at noon and practically all went home on their bicycles for dinner, instead of for lunch. The evening meal was supper.

They were summoned back to work by two blasts at quarter of one, with one blast at 1 o'clock. Its final act was to blow at 5 or 5 p.m. whichever hour happened to be the closing time.

The whistle was not in use when the company seemed to be going down hill and which was sold to the Kaiser-Fraser Company. The whistle was gone from the city before local residents were aware of it -- sold to a company in Springfield, Ohio.

20

P.D. Beckwith

Dowagiac was fortunate that Philo D. Beckwith decided to come to Dowagiac in 1854 for the community owes much to this vigorous, generous man.

Philo D. Beckwith was born in the Township of Pike, Allegany County, New York on March 6, 1825. This was newly settled country at the time and part of the Holland Purchase.

His father, Stephen Beckwith, was a cooper by trade. His mother was Narcissa Beach, daughter of Daniel Beach, an early settler in an adjoining township. Stephen died at the age of 40 and Narcissa at the age of 50.

Philo married Catherine Scott when he was 19 and she was 16. Five years later, in 1844, they came to Detroit, from there to Ypsilanti and the next year, 1851 to Michigan City; to Niles in 1852 and to Dowagiac in 1854. They had two daughters, Kate Beckwith who married Fred E. Lee, and Della who married Charles Gardner, parents of Archie Gardner.

He is believed to be the only man who had served both as village president and city mayor of Dowagiac, holding the latter office for a number of years.

He was popular with his employees and his help to persons in need was legendary. He supported everything for the public good and substantially with money. He erected a building for the Ladies Library Association and gave it to them.

Anything for the public good he supported, churches, concerts, lecture courses, all could count on him.

He loved to dance, and many said, he put a hard maple flooring in the old Round Oak warehouse for that purpose, and which was built beside what is now The Daily News building. Many dances were held there.

He loved music and the theater -- he loved life -- and lived a full but short one, dying in January 1889 at the age of 63. But his remains do not rest in Dowagiac where most of his life was spent -- but in Battle Creek where he once lived.

One street, a short block, Beckwith Ave., was named for him and that is all. The Beckwith building was his monument -- a memorial to him -- and now it is gone.

21

Farm Implements Made

Dowagiac was for many years, starting well over a century ago, a leading manufacturer of farm implements—and Philo D. Beckwith, inventor of the Round Oak stove—and the Dowagiac Creek had something to do with it. Beckwith had come here in 1854 and established a little foundry on South Front Street on the banks of the Dowagiac Creek.

Dowagiac was the scene and home of the manufacture of the first shoe or runner drills, and what this meant to the agricultural world back in the 1850's and 1860's is no longer remembered.

Farmers broadcast their grain by hand with sometimes spotty results. Occasionally one would rig up something for evener distribution of his precious seed.

One of these was John S. Gage of Wayne Township whose "Centennial Farm," marked with an 1876 boulder in the front yard on Gage Street, is now owned by the Lester Stover family.

Gage, a son of Ebenezer Gage, and nephew of Justus Gage, was a pioneer Wayne Township settler, and an early school teacher. He experimented by hollowing out a log and drilling holes at regular intervals in it, and pulled it across his wheat fields by horse power. It worked so well that he took the idea to P.D. Beckwith and the roller grain drill was born in this little foundry. Before this Gage had made several of the log seeders for his neighbors.

P.D. Beckwith bought an interest in Gage's invention, had it patented, improved and perfected it, and manufactured it beside the Dowagiac Creek. The roller grain drill became so popular that it revolutionized the method of sowing small grains, not only in this country but in other grain-growing parts of the world.

Not only were the first Round Oak stoves made beside the creek, but in addition were the shoe grain drills, an invention of William Tuttle, a cousin of James Heddon, and grandfather of the late Harry Tuttle of Dowagiac.

In 1868 Beckwith purchased two acres of ground beside the railroad tracks, and on the west side, the nucleus of what was later to become the Round Oak factory. Here he continued to manufacture the roller grain drill for many years along with his stoves and furnaces.

William Tuttle and J.P. Warner took over his old location beside the creek and many persons will remember the "Drill Works" buildings along South Front Street. The last trace of this once flourishing business disappeared in the 1970's when the building on South Front and Chestnut Street was razed to make room for the high rise, Chestnut Towers.

"Dowagiac Drills and Seeders Are the Leaders," was the slogan on the trademark of the Dowagiac Manufacturing Company also known as the Dowagiac Shoe Grain Drill Company.

This company came about through the invention of William Tuttle, who invented the shoe grain drill in about the year 1865. He had it patented in 1867, and the first drill was actually made in Shep Wheeler's blacksmith shop in Keeler, where the Tuttles and Heddons lived before coming here.

Tuttle's first drill had wooden shoes, covered with trim. Philo D. Beckwith cast for him the first iron shoes used. This was in 1866. The man who made the first drill for him, Shepard Wheeler, conceived the idea of covering the grain by the use of a chain. The first chains were made here by James Wheeler, a colored blacksmith.

John Crawford and Amos Knapp who at that time had a wood-working and repair shop, helped Tuttle with the manufacture of that first drill. Harry Tuttle owned the first patent papers issued to his grandfather.

The company buildings on the creek burned in 1872, with the exception of one building. William Tuttle had by this time gone into other businesses and J.P. Warner and several others rebuilt the company.

In 1880 Warner invented a spring tooth harrow, which was described in 1882 as "an implement on wheels that does the work of a cultivator and seeder combined, and can be used either with one or two horses."

In November, 1881 a stock company was organized with a capital of $50,000, for the purpose of manufacturing both the harrow and the shoe grain drill. It was the first stock company formed in Cass County to carry on manufacturing. New buildings were erected and the company prospered.

M.E. Morse was the first president; C.W. Vrooman, vice president; H.F. Kellogg, secretary; Daniel Lyle, treasurer; and J.P. Warner, superintendent of works. Other stockholders were James Atwood, Samuel Ingling, C.L. Fowle, Dr. H.S. McMaster, Richard Heddon, Gideon Gibbs, William Tuttle, Loren Warner, Cyrus Tuthill, B.L. Dewey, C. Fred Clarke, and Isaac B. Hendrick.

Abner Moon wrote that "fully half of the original stockholders did not live to see their hopes realized beyond a limited degree, but others experienced the satisfaction of starting and developing one of the largest factories of its kind in the world, one half of its product of which now goes to foreign countries and the goods better and more favorably known in South America than in North America." This was in 1911.

By 1888 the company concentrated its efforts on the wheat-growing sections of the northwest and in Canada. Today some western and Canadian museums contain implements made here in Dowagiac. Branch distributing points were established at Fargo N.D., Minneapolis; Aberdeen, S.D.; St. Louis; Kansas City, Mo.; Dallas, Texas; and Los Angeles, Calif.

At the 1893 World's Fair in Chicago exhibits included "the little 11-shoe machine for small farms up to the big 26-shoe, four-horse drill for the big farms like that of Oliver Dalrymple, who has about 50 of them in use on his mammoth Dakota farms."

By 1894 C.E. Lyle was president; F.W. Lyle was vice president; W.F. Hoyt, secretary; N.F. Choate, treasurer; and C.L. Fowle, sales manager. Its capital stock was still $50,000 and its plant covered a little over three acres of ground. This may be the answer to what happened to a good company with a superior product; failure to expand faster with more invested capital.

In 1894 there were 250 "skilled artisans" employed in the plant on South Front Street, and the company was turning out 10,000 drills a year. This may sound like a small operation but it was before the day of the huge assembly line plants. Each man knew his job and took pride in it.

The best of materials were used and the company prided itself on producing quality drills and seeders, and no salesman ever had to apologize to a customer on behalf of his Dowagiac firm. They had a right to be proud because, surprisingly enough, many of the old grain drills and seeders were still in use less than 20 years ago and are still valued by their owners who have small acreages.

But other companies were producing good farm machinery, too, and even though the local company continually improved its product, making larger and more efficient drills, they did not expand enough in order to compete with the companies which began manufacturing on a larger scale, such as International Harvester, etc. It has been reported that International Harvester tried to buy out the local company but its offer was refused.

A story was published in The Dowagiac Daily News on November 1, 1911 which stated: "The 30 years state charter of the Dowagiac Manufacturing Co., has just expired and an extension of another 30 years has been secured, with the new name of 'The Dowagiac Drill Company,' to take effect within a week.

"The purpose of the change in name is apparent as it now designates the particular kind of goods manufactured, and is in itself, an advertisement. The sign on the plant to be read by passengers on one of the most traveled railroads of the country will now convey to the reader's mind the fact that not only is it a manufacturing plant, but that grain drills are still built there, and the same is true of each signature and stationery heading.

When the drill was first made it was just called "shoe drill" and was the only one of its kind for several years, but various imitations came along and the name "Dowagiac Shoe Drill" was adopted.

The company later made other types of farm machinery, but stuck mainly to its basic drills, seeders and harrows. It went into the furnace business after World War I trying to keep "its head above water" but there were too many good furnaces being made here then.

William F. Hoyt, who began with the company in 1885 as bookkeeper, stayed with it until it was sold along with its patents in the 1930's to the Springfield, Ohio company which makes repairs for the old drills.

One thing the company never lost was its good name and reputation for making "the best grain drill on earth," and many good seeders and drills are still left doing duty to bear out this statement.

The Dowagiac community's only regret is that its stockholders and officers of years ago failed to expand and progress fast enough to keep up with the competition for it had the products with which to do it.

22

The Heddons

Many interesting people have lived in Dowagiac—but if I was forced to choose just one—it would be James Heddon. Inventor, manufacturer, newspaper man, poet, philosopher, apiarist, politician, James Heddon was all of these and more.

The best way to start with James Heddon is to let Bob Davis, a columnist on the old New York Sun introduce "Uncle Jimmy Heddon, Patron Saint of Surface Bait Anglers."

Davis was fishing at Moose Cove, Maine in 1905 where he first saw what was then described as "the floating bass plug, the topwater of the surface bait." Davis described this bait in detail and said "the trade name of this remarkable device, which transformed bass, pickerel and muskelunge angling from a tedious uncertain enterprise into an ecstatic joy was 'The Dowagiac,' commemorating a city of that name in the southwestern part of Michigan along the Michigan Central Railroad."

He said "I fell lock, stock and barrel for the Dowagiac surface bait. Its most attractive feature, that of requiring the fish to rise and make the strike on top of the water, put a veritable kick into the joys of fishing."

Davis began corresponding with Heddon who signed himself "Uncle Jimmy" and was invited to come to Dowagiac. "My first meeting with this remarkable man I shall long remember always with a poignant feeling that I am not ever to look upon him again, unless it be when I cross the Styx and find him with rod and reel strolling those mysterious shores."

"Leaving the train I mixed with the crowd, making my way slowly along the platform. Suddenly a small, gray, pixie-like man with two of the brightest eyes ever set in a human head, appeared at my side. 'Your name is Davis," he said quietly, 'I'm Heddon. Let's get out of this mob. Tomorrow you and I go fishing.' This was in 1906. Davis then described their trip to Potato Lake, Wis. by train, Ford car and Buckboard. Heddon talked about farming, cattle raising, fruit cultivation and bees, said Davis.

"There was no subject relating to nature with which he was not familiar. And when it came to the life of the bee, to which he had devoted his entire youth, he was better than Maurice Maeterlinck. Reveling in his vast knowledge, his flowing speech and his fine sense of humor, I was transported into the kingdom of the outdoors as never before."

The fishing was everything Heddon promised him. "When night fell, we turned off the babble that dealt with piscatology and went peacefully to bed.

"It was one of Uncle Jimmy's pleasures, weather permitting, to don his old-fashioned night shirt, step out on the porch and quote Tom Paine, Voltaire, Bob Ingersoll and sometimes Shakespeare and the poems of Robert Burns, with whom he was in tune. His selections were of the sort that made a listener aware of the imperishable beauty born of the human mind, and he could name a hundred poets and philosophers, stars of the first magnitude.

"For five years I fished with Uncle Jimmy Heddon, and because of his influence, found a better and saner view of life, a richer outlook on its turmoil and learned what makes friendships survive the grave."

James Heddon was born Aug. 28, 1845 in the Genesee Valley in eastern New York, the son of Mr. and Mrs. Richard Heddon. He died in Dowagiac on Dec. 11, 1911. His father, Richard Heddon, was born in 1818 in Devonshire, England, and was 12 years old when he came to the United States with his parents. In 1850 Richard Heddon and his family moved to Keeler Township in Van Buren County, and in 1860 to Dowagiac to live.

James Heddon and his father shared two interests, both served as mayors of Dowagiac, and it was Richard Heddon who established the Heddon Apiary, at one time the largest in the country. Richard

Heddon even tried his hand at making baits before his death in 1899.

But it was the casting plug that brought James Heddon lasting fame. He was inducted into the Sports Hall of Fame in 1956 as its inventor.

Today James Heddon & Sons Inc. is the only manufacturing concern still active in Dowagiac of all the many companies in business before and after the Heddon company was started. The Heddon company, part of a conglomerate for a number of years, is now locally owned.

How James Heddon came to invent the casting plus is one of those lucky accidents. Many stories have been written about it, not only locally but in sports magazines and newspaper columns. He was fishing one day on the Dowagiac Millpond, and apparently the fish were not biting with any great speed. He sat there whittling on a piece of wood. He tossed the chunk of wood into the water and a big bass leaped up after it. It didn't take Heddon's fertile mind long to realize he had something there.

He went home and carved from a piece of pine wood, a cigar-shaped lure to which he attached several hooks. He caught fish with it, and he soon began trying to perfect it.

The late Philip S. Johnson, a Grand Rapids newspaperman for many years, who was born at "Wilderness Farm" northeast of Dowagiac, wrote to Richard M. Judd Sr. in 1953. Johnson was working on The Dowagiac Times published by James Heddon and he was commandeered from time to time into rowing the boat during Heddon's experiments.

Johnson said that after he had put the paper to bed "I would drive him out to the mill pond with my horse and buggy and row a boat around the pond while he would flip various colored cedar plugs in the water to get the reaction of the fish to this kind of lure. He had plugs with every color of the rainbow and these experiments were really the start of the Heddon fish bait business." That was the end of Johnson's involvement with the casting plug as that fall he went to Chicago where Hugh Fullerton, city editor of The Chicago Tribune put him on the staff as a cub reporter.

Heddon kept experimenting and perfecting his lure and it wasn't too long before the family kitchen became a miniature factory, with

Mrs. Heddon and sons, Charles and Will making and painting lures.

Sales were a little slow at first, it is reported, but they soon picked up and the business outgrew the Heddon home at 401 Green Street. He moved his little factory into the Pray building which stood at the corner of South Front Street and Park Place. A few years later a factory was built at the site where the Heddon Factory is today.

While still working in the Heddon home they were experiencing difficulty in getting the paint to dry faster. Mrs. Heddon suggested baking them in the oven. Charles had painted lacquer over the paint hoping to make it dry. They were in a hurry to dry the baits as they were to be taken to a jobbers' meeting.

When baked in the oven the lacquer dried but it cracked and checked into little crevices. But Charles took the checked baits anyhow and introduced them as Heddon's new and special deluxe "crackleback" finish. It went over big and many orders were received. The bait is still made.

The company was formally organized in 1902 while Charles and Will were still with the company.

Robert Page Lincoln writing in the May, 1949 issue of "Outdoor" magazine wrote: "Effective as top-water plugs are during those hours when bass are feeding near shore, the fishing fraternity also needed a lure or plug that would go down for them when they are in water 15 or 20 feet deep. Answering this demand the Heddon company brought out their deep-running River Runt, with a metal scoop or mouthpiece which carries the lure downward at an angle of 45 degrees. In lakes where bass lie deep down in the summer a lure of this kind takes fish when surface baits are useless."

In closing, Lincoln who was also writing about other companies and other baits, said: "All in all, plug fishing is great sport and leads so far over all other methods of fishing as to make this type of lure the great American favorite. There may be equals to it in bass fishing, but no superiors. And Jim Heddon started it all with a piece of discarded wood."

James Heddon lived long enough to see his company carry his name around the world and to become a friend of many famous people of his day. Besides Bob Davis of the New York Sun, another close friend was Irvin S. Cobb, who visited him and wrote about him a number of times.

Heddon - The Beekeeper

There are thousands of people all over the world who are still familiar with the name of James Heddon—not because of the casting plug—unless they are fisherman—but through bees.

His father, Richard Heddon established his apiary on what is now Tuthill Street about 1869 and James learned the business from him. It was James who built up the business until the 1880's he was the leading honey producer in the United States; was editor of bee journals; and author of a book on bee culture.

Thanks to E.C. Martin, professor of entomology at Michigan State University, practically everything known about James Heddon as an apiarist, was furnished by him in 1970. I have a number of pages xeroxed from old bee journals, including the British Bee Journal which he provided. They show pictures of his inventions for the culture of the bee, including the Heddon have and slatted honey board.

By the 1800's James Heddon was internationally known for his many inventions and innovations connected with bee culture. He was assisted in publishing bee journals by Abner Moon.

Today no one can produce a single copy locally of anything he wrote about bees, including his book, "Success in Bee Culture," which he wrote in 1885.

He progressed from bees to the newspaper business. A life long Democrat he began editing The Dowagiac Times in the 1880's. The Dowagiac Daily News was "born" in The Times office in 1897, shortly after Heddon had turned the management of The Times over to his 19-year old son, Charles. By this time he had become involved in the manufacture of the casting plug.

Although Heddon's innovations in beekeeping many be passe today, they were still in vogue as late as 1917 and possibly longer. He developed the strain of Heddon bees which are still in existence and known to beekeepers.

Professor Martin also sent a summary of James Heddon's bee activities as recorded at Cornell University, not dated, except it was written after his death in 1911. It stated he commenced beekeeping in 1869 and in 1879 commenced dealing in hives and appliances. "Was one of the first to make a specialty of beekeeping—had as many as 600 colonies in his apiaries. Inventor of Heddon hive and slatted honey board.

"Was a prolific writer to the beekeepers. Took an interest in local affairs, edited The Dowagiac Times and in 1885 wrote "Success in Bee Culture.' " It went on to say the book was written after 17 years in connection with beekeeping, mostly in comb-honey production.

"It was written, not for the beginner, but the established beekeeper as he believed the business was becoming overcrowded." And not one word about casting plugs or lures.

The other Heddons

The sons of James Heddon, Charles and Will, were versatile as was their father. Their mother was Eva Hastings, and their grandfather was Charles Hastings who platted an addition to Dowagiac. Hastings Street is named for him.

Will Heddon was not entirely devoted ot the bait company as was his brother, Charles. It was Charles who picked up the reins from his father, James, and built up and expanded the Heddon Company.

Will, the younger of the two sons, early broke away from the Heddon Company management. He organized the Heddon Telephone Company in this city and which was highly successful, and which he later sold to the Bell Company. He moved to Florida and was established in business there.

Charles Heddon as 65 years old when he died in December, 1941, less than 24 hours after he left his desk at the Heddon offices.

he was president of the Dowagiac Daily News Company at the time of his death. In his obituary written by the publisher, Harry H. Whiteley, he said: "Charles Heddon's flair for organization and his business genius, as well as the superior products of the company, were in a great measure responsible for the success of his company, which is one of the city's leading industries, and one of the largest of its kind in the world.

"He was equally active in other fields in spite of the demands made upon his time by his own business interests. For years he was a devotee of billiards, holding a world's championship in the amateur field and playing regularly in amateur tournaments. He organized the Recreation Company in Detroit, a whole block devoted to billiards and bowling."

It was Will Heddon who made the first parachute jump in Dowagiac from a hot-air filled balloon, according to the May 12, 1892 issue of the old Dowagiac Republican: "Will Heddon, the boy aeronaut, made a balloon ascension and parachute leap from the park in this city last Saturday that, without a doubt, was the most successful ever made in this part of the country. One of the Baldwin Brothers of Quincy, Ill., came here and made all the arrangements and sent him off in the finest kind of shape.

"When about a mile in height he struck a strong current of wind that appeared at first as though it would capsize the balloon. After ascending about a mile and a half he cut loose from the balloon, shooting downward like a shot for about 400 feet, when the parachute opened up, bearing him downward very gracefully, landing near G.S. Wilbur's (Wilbur Hill) about three-fourths of a mile from his starting place."

The Republican said the ascent occupied two minutes and the descent two minutes and 10 seconds, "by the watch.

"This was said by those posted in aeronautics to be the highest hot air balloon ascension ever made in the country."

Five generations of Heddons have lived in Dowagiac, now there are none, and like many other pioneer families, their descendants are scattered all over the country.

Sugar-mining

In 1916 W.H. Tuttle of Decatur wrote a letter to The Decatur Republican telling of sugar making 50 years before with his "Cousin Jim" who was none other than James Heddon of Dowagiac.

There was a woodlot on the Tuttle farm in Hamilton Township with about 30 maple trees and every spring his Cousin Jim would come from Dowagiac to help him make maple sugar and maple syrup.

"My mother would contribute the kettles in which to boil the sap and we would have a few weeks of perfect happiness. We got our 30 trees tapped, troughs hewed out, the stove kettles hung up next to a large log and were ready to do business when the sap began to run.

"To complete our happiness father hitched up his team one day and drew a small load of lumber from his mill to our camp and showed us how tomake a small hut. We took some of the shorter boards and set them up endways in the shape of a tent and then boarded up the back tightly leaving the front open facing the fire. We got some straw from the barn for the floor and if we weren't happy no one was.

"We had potatoes to roast in the ashes and meat to cook on sticks and mother saw to it we had plenty of pies and cookies. We each had a gun and all we had to do was to keep the sap boiling, lie on the straw in front of the fire and read Beadle's Dime Novels and occasionally go squirrel hunting. In planning our future lives Jim and I decided to be Indian fighters, hunters and trappers somewhere out in the unknown west.

"For all of our lack of modern conveniences we made some very good sugar and syrup. Sugaring off day—about once a week—was a great event. Then we would take all of the thin syrup we had made during the week and boil it down again until it was thick enough to grain and pour it into pans and stir it until it solidified and we would have the nicest fine white maple sugar, fit for a feast.

"Jim and I made sugar that way for several seasons, then my people moved to town. Jim had to go to work and I had to go to school and the little sugar bush and our hut was left to themselves. The trees were all cut down and sold. I do not know what became of the hut, but the last time I saw the place it was a cleared field.

"Jimmy is dead and I am left to think it over, once in a while and regret that I cannot go back and live it over once more. Those were great and glorious days to us two boys and they beat being grown up a long ways."

23

Oldest Public Building

The oldest public building in Dowagiac is St. Paul's Episcopal Church on Courtland. Built in 1859 it was then the Universalist Church and was also used as the city's auditorium. It had the first pipe organ in the community and which was in use until recent years.

Almost everything of a public nature happened here. As one elderly citizen remarked years ago, "if only its walls could speak -- what tales it could tell" of the many famous people whose voices were heard there. Dowagiac being located on the Michigan Central made this city a natural stopping place and also contained many residents who were appreciative of the opportunity to hear people "from the outside world."

The old Cass County Republican of Oct. 22, 1874 reported: "The Universalist Church was well filled last Thursday evening to listen to Susan B. Anthony's lecture on Woman Suffrage. Her argument was lengthy but not particularly convincing being mostly a repetition of such arguments as have been previously advanced by those in favor of the movement, and elicited but little enthusiasm.

"At the close she asked all voters to respond 'aye' or 'no' as they intended to at the polls in November, and then asked the ladies to vote 'aye' or 'no' as they wished the question carried or not. Singular as it may seem, both were carried in the affirmative."

Two women candidates for president over 100 years ago, Belva Lockwood and Victoria Woodhull both spoke in the Universalist Church and attracted big audiences.

The church was visited by some of the world's greatest artists of their day, among them, Ole Bull, the violinist; John B. Gough, impersonator; and Theresa Carreno, who was conceded at that time to be the world's foremost pianist.

And these were only a very few of the famous people who came here. The community also used the building for entertainments of all kinds.

Two different times it has housed school classes, including the German Lutheran School.

When it was remodeled some years ago its hand hewn beams, square hand-made nails were much appreciated by builders and carpenters who worked on this well constructed building.

The church was idle for some years; was occupied by St. Albans' Episcopal Church; and after another period of idleness, was deeded to St. Paul's Episcopal Church.

The oldest store building on Commercial Street was razed when The Dowagiac Savings Association expanded through the block to the alley. Built in 1849, it was moved from its location beside the railroad to Commercial St. Its last occupants were The Dowagiac Pastry Shop and the Scott Insurance Agency.

The buildings on the west side of Front Stret, or most of them are over a century old.

The oldest home may be that of Mr. and Mrs. Irving Johnson at 114 Cross St. The oldest brick building is the old ReShore home now owned by H.D. Klingaman at 208 West Division. It was built in 1848 or 1849.

24

First Schools

To Dowagiac belongs the distinction of opening the first tax-supported public school in the state west of Detroit and Monroe. This was in 1840. There were of course, other schools in the state and Cass County prior to that time, but they were supported by subscription. If parents couldn't contribute anything to the support of the school, their children didn't go.

On April 18, 1840, the school inspectors of the townships of LaGrange, Pokagon, Silver Creek and Wayne met in the home of Patrick Hamilton, then a farm home in Silver Creek. There was no Dowagiac then, just a little settlement along the mill dam as Justus Gage reported when he drove through here in 1837 to his land in Wayne Township on what is now the Rudy Road.

There were enough people living in the community to warrant opening a school.

These inspectors included Alexander H. Redfield, Benjamin Gould and John G. Mitchell of LaGrange; Justus Gage, Ebenezer Gage and William M. Barney of Wayne; James Selleck, Eli N. Veach and James S. Doster of Silver Creek; and Lewis Edwards and Henry Houser of Pokagon Township.

They organized District No. 4. They chose the number, four, because there were four townships involved. It was called a Silver Creek Township School because that was the township in which it was located.

It was a little one-room log school and built just east of the present Heddon factory building on what was later the site of the old City

Cemetery.

The first teacher was Hannah Compton, and the Hamilton, McOmber and other children of pioneer families went to school here. Miss Compton, who afterwards married Elias Jewell, was said not to spare the rod.

It only lasted a few terms, some becomeing dissatisfied "with the morals of the pupils and others insisting that public schools bred rascality and immorality rather than virtue." They withdrew their children and the school broke up. The school was on land belonging to Patrick Hamilton and he moved the building nearer to his home and used it for a granary.

The community then went back to the select or private school system, although some did attend Wayne Township School No. 9, later known as the Dutch or Chiverton School just outside the east city limits of Dowagiac. Some children continued to attend private schools even when the public school was available. Two of them open during this period was one taught by a Miss Copley in what then known as the "Cataract House," a railroad boarding house on the bluff in the vicinity of High and South Front Streets Miss Mary Buell taught a private school from 1854 to 1856 in her home just west of the old Baptist Church which was located on the corner of Center and Spruce Streets.

Others attended a private school taught by Mrs. Henry C. Hills about a half-mile from the city, now the Sedlar farm home and once the home of King C. Gillette and his family. Mrs. Hills' sister, Miss Cheeseborough, looked after the household duties while her sister was teaching.

However Dowagiac was not long without a public school and in 1850 a one-story frame school house was built on the site of the former First Methodist Church on New York and Commerical Street.

There was but one teacher at first but the town was growing fast and it became necessary to have two teachers. The late Flavia Defendorf, who came to Dowagiac in 1852, remembered attending school there. Boys sat on one side of the room and girls on the other. They apparently were taking no chances on the students' morals this time.

Among the teachers in this school were Mrs. Keables, Orrin T.

Welch, Miss Abbie Simmons, who afterwards became Mrs. Welch, Miss Louisa Fuller, and Miss Nellie Thomas who afterwards married F.J. Atwell, Dowagiac's first mayor; also A.D.P. Van Buren. Others were Lucinda Hotchkiss of Niles and Anna Lee.

The building was also used by the Congregationalists on Sunday morning and the Methodists Sunday afternoon. The Methodists later purchased it and moved it to another location on New York Avenue. It was reported that it was again used for school purposes for a couple of years, and eventually burned down.

This one story frame school house soon became inadequate and in the year 1856 a two-story frame building was erected in the western part of the village. Many were opposed to a school being built out in the oak grubs, many predicting "the town will never grow that far," and that it was inconvenient of access. This is the school which burned down in September, 1859.

Other school buildings have been constructed through the years, old Central School in 1861; the four-room Ward School on the site of the present Justus Gage School in 1864, followed by the high school building, which also contained grades, opened in 1904; McKinley school in 1904; old Lincoln School in 1913 converted from the old Joel Smith home, and a number of other buildings in recent years. However Union High School is the first building in all these years constructed exclusively for high school use.

25

First School Board

The first school board of record was that of 1848, the same year the village was platted, and consisted of Ira Mosher, president; Henry C. Wells, director; and Patrick Hamilton, director.

In 1853 there were seven trustees: Isaac Cross, president; James M. Spencer, director; Ira Starkweather, assessor; and Gilman Jones, Patrick Hamilton, I.S. Becraft and E. Ballingee, trustees.

Board members fluctuated constantly, going back to a 3-man board in 1857 and two years later again increased to seven.

In 1887 there were six: Gideon Gibbs, president; W.K. Palmer, director; Daniel Lyle, treasurer; T.W. Adams, Cyrus Tuthill and Burgette L. Dewey, trustees.

In the year of 1877, when Dowagiac was incorporated as a city, this also changed the school setup. For the first time there was a superintendent of schools and he was C.O. Tower, with Miss Addie M. Ingersoll as the principal. He was followed by M.W. Smith, J.W. Simmons, J.R. Miller, and S.B. Laird who reigned for quite a few years until Warren E. Conkling took over in 1897.

Principals were all women from 1877 on. Besides Miss Ingersoll there was Miss Frances Wall, Miss Libbie McElroy, Miss Nettie M. Dally, until George W. Green became principal in 1897. He also served as football coach and afterwards went to medical school and better known as Dr. George W. Green to citizens of today.

District No. 4, organized in 1840 included Section 31 in Wayne; Sections 1 and 2 and the east half of section 3 in Pokagon Township; sections 25, 26, 35, 36 and the east half of Sec. 34, also the east part of the southeast half of Sec. 27 lying on the east side of the "big" Dowagiac Creek all in Silver Creek; and the north half of the northeast quarter of Sec. 6 in LaGrange all made up this district.

This district shrunk considerably as more settlers moved into the area and rural schools were established closer to their homes. Some time after 1848 the district was reorganized as Union District No. 1, a name it has retained ever since, with the exception of a change in number to 31 in recent years by the Intermediate School District. It retained portions of Pokagon, Silver and LaGrange which were close to the village limits. Wayne was not a part of the Union District until recent years.

Annexation in recent years has greatly enlarged the boundaries, and it has for Marcellus. Cassopolis and Edwardsburg school districts in the rest of the county. Cass County is now composed of four high school districts.

26

High School

The Dowagiac community has an enviable educational record, due no doubt to the many New Englanders who settled here in the city's earliest days. Dowagiac had a high school before it was incorporated as a village which is a good indication of the kind of people who lived here. Dowagiac shares with Niles the honor of having the first high school in southwestern Michigan. It opened Nov. 2, 1857.

Before that many residents sent their children east to be educated, usually back to a community from which they came and where they could live with relatives.

Dowagiac, however had a form of a high school, the Young Ladies Seminary. Where it was located has never been determined. It was established here some time in the early 1850's. A.D.P. Van Buren wrote about this school in the Michigan Pioneer Collections. He said: "Miss H. Marie Metcalf of Battle Creek had started the Young Ladies school at Dowagiac, but soon found it so large that she sought help, consequently I was requested to take charge as principal, which I did on Oct. 4, 1856, she becoming assistant.

"The village of Dowagiac was then seven years old, had some 1,200 inhabitants, two churches, four taverns, and stores enough to accommodate the surrounding country.

"The school was composed of girls from the age of 20 down to the child of seven or eight years. These, with some 10 or 12 boys, to favor certain parents, constituted our charge. After we had taught a quarter of the term, the directors of the school district made arrangements with us to take charge of the Union school, which the people of Dowagiac were about to organize. Hence our program was changed, and I was to be the one to call the school clans together here, as I had done six years before in Battle Creek, and form them into a union school."

Owing to the fact that the school records were burned in the fire of 1859, there seems to be a conflict in Van Buren's statement about organizing the union school. However there was some type of graded system in the 1850's and this may have been what he was referring to in his statement.

In the obituary of Justus Gage in the Cass County Republican of Feb. 4, 1875, it states that "in the fall of 1860 he was chosen director of the village school of Dowagiac, and proceeded at once to the inauguration of the Union or graded school system under the free school law. During the six succeeding years, in connection with the school board, he succeeded in raising the schools of the town to so high a reputation as to gain for them the praise of beging model schools of the state."

A new school building had been erected on the site of the present Central Junior High School in 1856 and this, coupled with the fact that Van Buren was principal of the Young Ladies Seminary, may have accounted for some change in school operations.

This building "is pleasantly situated in a grove of two acres, in a retired part of town." So wrote Principal H.S. Jones in his report to Ira Mayhew, State Superintendent of Public Instruction, dated Jan. 13, 1858. His report is on file in the State Archives in Lansing.

As no known picture of this first building used as a high school, his description is unvaluable. "A main part is 32 by 54, two stories in height. The main building is divided into three departments, two of which are on the ground floor.

"They are first primary, second primary, grammar school and high school. Number of teachers employed, four: One male teacher as principal; the residue, females. The expenses for instruction will be about $1,100 for the school year. The average number of scholars in attendance at this date, "one hundred and eighty."

"The age of this institution will not allow a very favorable report respecting advanced students. A number are studying the

Languages with the intention of entering the State University as soon as prepared. (Some did without the formality of commencement exercises).

"The high school commences with Higher Arithmetic, Grammar, Composition, Analysis of English sentence, Declamation, Elocution, Spelling and Defining. The Course extends through three years embracing all the branches mostly taught at Academies and High Schools.

In a short report made the following year, Prof. Jones listed "instumental music" as one of the subjects being taught.

He said that the high school barely two months old, "as yet the apparatus necessary for an institution of this kind has not been purchased, though there is good reason to believe that the deficiency will be supplied at an early day.

"Discipline is mild but firm, founded on the self-control of both teachers and students.

"My experience leads me to be decidedly in favor of the co-education of the sexes. The influence of each sex on the other is of a pleasant and healthy character, when properly controlled by the teacher. The co-education of the sexes begets, on the one part, neatness, gentleness and respect; on the other, all that makes the body, based on self-reliance and energy of character."

This school burned down in the fall of 1859 on a Friday evening about a week or two after school had been in session. Students were scattered in buildings throughout the town, the high school in the old ReShore building, which later burned, the intermediate department in a cooper shop.

A new brick school opened on this site in 1861, and here the city's second high school was conducted. Two wings were added in the 1880's and many live in this community who attended grade school and junior high school here. This was the old Central School.

Dowagiac's third high school opened in 1904 on the site of the present Justus Gage School, and later became the Oak Street School when Central High School, now a junior high school, was opened in 1926.

The present Union High School, the academic wing of which opened in the fall of 1961, is Dowagiac's fifth high school in almost

125 years.

Latin, Greek and German were taught in the high school for many years. Greek was dropped around 1900 for the lack of instructors. German was dropped during World War I, and French was substituted. Spanish was added to the curriculum later. Physics and chemistry were added in the 1800's.

Agriculture was introduced some years before World War I. The commercial department was opened in the early 1900's with the late A.R. Mead as its first department head. Domestic science, as home economics was first called, and manual training were also added some years before World War I.

During the earlier years there was a strong emphasis on literature and the high school students of those days was very familiar with Shakespeare as well as other classical authors, along with debating and elocution. There was a keen interest among the adults of the community, and a knowing and critical audience greeted the efforts of the young people who performed in public, usually the Universalist Church, now St. Paul's Episcopal Church, then the town's only auditorium. Shakespearean and literary clubs were popular among the students.

No one knows when athletics started but the first local field meet was held here in 1886. Baseball predominated for many years among young and old. Football began in the 1890's. Tennis courts were built beside the high school building in 1904 when it was first opened. The football and baseball diamond were interchangeable, surrounded by a cinder track. How well old time football players remember having their noses ground into those cinders as the result of a hard tackle.

27

High School Graduation

Dowagiac's first formal Commencement program took place in April, 1864. This was seven years after the high school opened. The first class should have graduated in 1860, but was hampered by the fire of 1859. However oldtime stories have mentioned persons "graduating" from Dowagiac High school prior to that time.

There were three graduates in 1864, Isaac R. Dunning, Lottie Hills and Hattie Smead.

Thanks to Belle Allmendinger Vrooman, the diploma of Isaac R. Dunning has been preserved. Mrs. Vrooman, a former resident of Benton Harbor, was visiting friends there, in the former Dunning home. She gave Mrs. Vrooman the diploma and some pictures taken in the old O.B. Dunning studio in this city.

The diploma provided some information that was formerly unknown. The heading states: "Dowagic Graded School, High School Department. To whom it may concern: Greeting. This certified that Isaac R. Dunning has completed the course of study prescribed by the rules and regulations of the Dowagiac Graded School, with commendable standing and deportment, and is entitled to the privilege of graduation which he hereby granted.

"Given under our sanction at Dowagiac, Michigan, this First day of April, Anno Domini 1864. Board of Trustees: Dan'l Larzelere, president; Justus Gage, secretary; Daniel Lyle, Gideon Gibbs, H.F. Colby, G.S. Wilbur.

At the left was listed the teachers: C.L. Whitney, principal, Juliet Bradbury, M.J. Jordan, and A.C. Wall, and signed at the bottom by

C.L. Whitney, principal. Each teacher signed, as did the trustees.

It was an important occasion, not only to the student, but to the entire community.

28

The Bible

Carefully preserved on the shelves of Union High School Library, is a book which has been the property of the Dowagiac schools for over a century. It is a Bible presented by the "Young Ladies of the High and Grammar School Department.

In beautiful handwriting inscribed on the front page it says: "Presented to the Dowagiac Graded School by the Young Ladies of the High and Grammar School Department, Oct. 9, 1865.

"Names of Donors: (Mr. Alward $1.10); Josie Harris, 65; Lydia Hebron, 60; Laura Felt, 50; Marcia Buck, 50; Nellie Cady, 15; Mary Thomas 65; Anna Breese, 65; Fannie Hebron, 25; Jane Hebron, 34; Mattie McNair, 55; Annie Fraser, 25; Maggie Cullom, 50; Martha Bedford, 25.

Mary Pattison, 30; Dellie Beckwith, 25; Clara Sullivan, 30; Emma Vanderhoof, 25; Sarah Barney, 25; Ella Bird, 25; Mary Cullom, 25; Stella Jewell, 25; Maggie Snyder, 25; Rozilla Walter, 25; Amelia Spencer, 25; Ella Carver, 25; Bevvie Fletcher, 25; Josie Lillie, 50; Maria Hallock, 50; Amelia Ellis, 50; total, $12.00.

The Bible was published by the New York Bible Society in 1863.

29

Dowagiac Churches

Churches in Dowagiac 100 years ago were not as many as there are today. The First Baptist Church erected the first church building here in 1852. It was organized in the summer of 1851 with the assistance of the Rev. S.H.D. Vaughn, and who was its first resident pastor. Before that the Rev. Jacob Price, a Baptist minister, was the first one to preach in Dowagiac, in the Michigan Central freight house.

The Rev. Richard C. Meek, a Methodist, was the first of his denomination to preach here, in the old "Cataract House," and in the Railroad House. In the beginning Dowagiac was a part of a big circuit. Some circuit preachers were said to have been here as early as 1843 but their names are unknown.

The first Methodist church building was erected in 1859 on New York and Commercial St.

The Congregational Church was established in 1849 by the Rev. Sidney Smith Brown who organized a society in the home of Patrick Hamilton. The first church was constructed in 1856. The Congregational Church joined with the First Baptist in 1918 to form the present Federated Church.

The Universalist Church was organized in 1858 and the present St. Paul's Episcopal Church building, was built in 1859, and dedicated in January, 1860. It went out of existence many years ago, and Episcopalians took it over in 1898, and again in the 1900's.

The first Episcopal service was conducted here in 1852, by the Rev. Joseph Phillips, rector of Trinity Church, Niles. He was the grandfather of Ring Lardner.

While the Roman Catholic Church was the first in this area, Dowagiac Catholics went to Silver Creek to church until 1872, when they built a church on Prairie Ronde Street, adjoining the present Calvary Cemetery. It was called "The Church of the Holy Maternity." This served the community until the 1890's when the present Holy Maternity of Mary Church was built.

Father John Cappou of Niles was the first priest to serve as pastor of the first Catholic church here.

The First Christian Church was organized in 1875, and erected its present church building at Oak and McOmber Streets in 1876.

There was a Presbyterian Society here at one time but they never established a church. They met on Sundays in the old school house on New York and Commercial.

30

Ladies Library Association

The Ladies Library Association is the oldest organization in Dowagiac that has been in continuous operation. It was formally organized and chartered on April 9, 1872. However a reading room had been in existence for some time before that. Dowagiac also had a book and stationary store from the early 1850's.

The association was brought to life in Young Men's Hall on the second floor of the present Phillipson store. At this meeting they adopted a constitution and by-laws which provided for a board of nine elected directors and dedicated itself to the support of the library.

This first board included Mrs. Gilman C. Jones, Mrs. Samuel Johnson, Mrs. F.J. Atwell, Mrs. W.K. Palmer, Mrs. Spafford Tryon, Mrs. P.S. Mulvane, Mrs. E.C. Chappell, Mrs. P.D. Beckwith and Miss Florence Cushman.

Mrs. Jones was chosen as the first president; Mrs. Johnson, vice president; Mrs. Tryon, corresponding secretary; Mrs. Atwell, recording secretary; Mrs. Mulvane, treasurer; and Miss Cushman, librarian.

Listed as charter members were: Maria Palmer, Amanda W. Jones, Mary E. Lyle, Mrs. H.D. Bowling, Mrs. Lurany B. Dickson, Mary W. Sherwood, Emma E. Van Riper, Gertrude ReShore, Jerusia E. Baily, Caroline J. Mulvane and Lillie A. Curtis.

Organized as a corporate body, the members set the capital stock at $1,000, divided into $2 shares and canvassed the city for subscribers. Some 200 shares were sold and with this money the group ordered the first stock of books "from the east."

The Ladies Library Association in the first few years, rented or borrowed rooms, but as it grew more room was badly needed. In 1888 P.D. Beckwith erected a building on the Front Street, between Pine Street and West Division. He had intended to establish a park on this lot. "We are pleased to notice that the Ladies Library Association is now in a good position on the triangular lot just east of Sherwood's" reported The Dowagiac Times of Nov. 7, 1889.

This was Dowagiac's library until the early 1900's when members of the association heard of Andrew Carnegie's offer to build public libraries. They persuaded the city council to pass the necessary resolution which it did on Jan. 9, 1903.

All that was needed was a suitable site, and the members went out after it. They urged William G. Howard and Fred E. Lee, trustees of the P.D. Beckwith estate, to deed two lots at the corner of Commerical St. and New York Avenue, which they did. While construction was in progress they gave the use of their building for a public library and started work on cataloguing their collection of nearly 3,000 books which they donated to the public library.

As soon as the new library opened, they closed theirs, and rented the building. For 44 years it brought in about $1,000 a year, the money being used to buy books for the public library.

While Robert J. Weller was mayor some 25 years ago, he thought it about time that the city bought the books for the library and not lean so heavily on the Ladies Library Association. The council agreed with him and that is the way it has been ever since.

After the old building was razed, the association has rented the site as a parking lot. Proceeds from this rental is still used for the benefit of the library, as well as membership dues. Members also raise funds in other ways.

31

Fire Department

The Fourth of July has always had a special significance for Dowagiac and particularly for the Dowagiac Fire Department. It was on July 4, 1860, that its old fire engine, a 10-inch Cowing hand pumper, set a world's record for distance at Battle Creek during a firemen's muster.

The record still exists in the New England record books although an eastern city has tried to claim the title—but the record is there to stay for all time. And the Dowagiac Fire Department proudly displays a silver firemen's trumpet suitably engraved with its record, 281 feet and 7 inches.

Dowagiac will be ever grateful to Charles N. Barnard, who was editor of TRUE Magazine in July 1953, who uncovered the record and wrote a story of these events. There were many local stories extant concerning this event but no one here knew that a world's record had been made by a little village on the Michigan Central over a century ago. And it looks as if the record for throwing water will stand for all time unless another old hand "tub" comes along that can beat it.

This is the way TRUE magazine reported it: "The world's record for horizontal play by a hand-pumped engine stands at 281 feet, 7 inches, set by the Hamilton Company of Dowagiac, Michigan, with a 10-inch Cowing machine on July 4, 1860," stated Barnard. There's other proof he stated, kept in old leather-bound ledgers since the first official record was made at a muster in Bath, Maine on July 4, 1849. These ledgers are in New England where old fashioned firemen's musters are occasionally held, and cherished old fire engines are brought out to spout water once more in competition.

In 1960, when The Daily News put out a special edition honoring the fire department, John F. Cutter Sr., "whose mind contains the history of firemen's musters for two generations," was secretary of the New Egland Veteran Fireman's League, which also has the records. Up to 1960 there had been over 1,000 official firemen's musters held in over a century. A muster includes several engines in competition, a contest between two engines does not count.

The old hand-pumped engine, which had served Dowagiac so long and faithfully, was sold in 1893 to a North Dakota town for $250 and the city throught it was lucky to get rid of the "old mankiller." Even though it took 30 to 40 men to operate her, she was spouting water while the magnificient new steamer was still clearing its throat, and did not require half the pampering.

And there is no steamer in the world which has ever beaten or even equalled the record she made that hot Fourth of July day in Battle Creek, in what is now the nation's oldest competitive sport—the firemen's muster. And neither has any modern 1,000 gallon-a-minute gasoline-powered pumper. It has been tried.

They tried it at the International Fire Chief's convention in Boston over 20 years ago. They lined up a gasoline pumper, an Amoskeag steamer (Dowagiac had an Amoskeag for a few momths) and a Columbia hand tub.

The Amoskeag steamer threw a longer stream that Boston's modern enginer—"and the hand tub Columbia licked 'em both hands down." And Dowagiac "sold down the river," the Cowing, the greatest hand tub of them all.

Dowagiac's fire department was still in its infancy in 1858, the year the village was incorporated and elected Justus Gage as its first village president. It was at a village council meeting on Nov. 10, 1858 that it was decided to purchase a fire engine. He appointed Hervey Bigelow, Ira Brownell and Joel Smith as a committee.

During that winter, early in 1859, they decided upon a 10-inch Cowing, the largest obtainable which they purchased of Cowing & Co. of Seneca Falls, N.Y. "with all the necessary appliances." The cost was $1,200. At the same time a fire house was constructed on

West Division Street to house the engine and razed some years ago when the present fire station was built. In 1882 it was still going strong and described as "the excellent hand engine still in use."

A volunteer fire company was organized, "Hamilton Fire Company No. 1," named after Patrick Hamilton, one of the village's foremost citizens. The local fire laddies were so proud of their engine that the next year, 1860 they decided to go and compete in the firemen's muster at Battle Creek.

The New England states in the east, and Michigan in the middle west, were the two greatest centers for firemen's musters. TRUE magazine reported musters usually ended in fights and brawls. Early on the morning of July 4, 1860, the Cowing pumper was loaded on a Michigan Central flat car and hauled to Battle Creek. Battle Creek's streets were very sandy and the firemen had difficulty in pulling their engine to the scene of action. Niles firemen were reported to have come to their aid as they did later.

Every town along the Michigan Central that had a company was represented, and some had steamers which were already coming into vogue. Detroit sent 100 men and was said to have a steamer. James Onen, who was still a resident of Niles in 1860, before moving to Dowagiac, suggested to his men that they help out the Hamiltons who were apparently a little short of manpower. Old stories say that the Detroit team was overbearing and bound to win at any cost, and apparently bullied the judges who gave them first place, although they later reversed themselves.

Saloons ran wide open and firemen usually "tanked up" both themselves and their machines and it didn't take much to start a brawl. It was no doubt responsible for what happened later.

After Detroit was awarded first prize, Dowagiac indignantly refused to accept second prize—as the record was there for all to see, 281 feet and 7 inches. When the judges reversed themselves, arguments arose.

Jesse Johnson, a member of the team, and whose son later became sheriff of Berrien County, "put several of the Detroit men to sleep," in the Donnybrook that followed. As near as can be learned all the Dowagiac firemen came home in one piece.

When Dowagiac residents heard of their fire department's great victory, "half the town boarded the first train and went down to help share in the honor. A dance was gotten up that evening and the Dowagiac firemen were not allowed to spend a cent for anything." And today no one knows who it was who unfairly awarded first prize to Detroit.

The names of that team have been lost, but Daniel Huff, one of its members recalled in 1913 that John O'Donoghue, Peter Hannan and Jesse Johnson were among them.

Some time later the Cowing Company presented the Hamilton Company of Dowagiac with the silver firemen's trumpet inscribed with the record and the fact that the Dowagiac company had refused second prize when it had rightfully won first prize.

The trumpet was carefully preserved by the late A.B. Gardner, grandson of P.D. Beckwith, and his son, the late Jack Gardner, returned it to Dowagiac. Wayne Clark had a walnut case built for it and for several years it was on display in the Dowagiac library before being turned over to the Dowagiac Fire Department.

How Records Were Made

Charles N. Barnard in the July, 1953 issue of TRUE magazine described how a water throwing competition is conducted at a firemen's muster. He said that many vertical-play records have been made but none are considered as accurate as the horizontal record.

The measuring platform he said, "is a strip of brown building paper laid flat on a base of boards and must be 9 feet wide and 150 feet long, thus providing for the measurement of a stream of water up to 275 feet from the tip of a nozzle." Apparently they do not expect to better Dowagiac's record of 281 feet any more.

After each "try" during a 15-minute period, the dozen officials, and all experienced old timers, move to the point where the last drop of "solid water" has landed, circle it with a crayon, measure its distance, then record it. Spray or mist doesn't count.

Barnard quoted John Cutter as saying that all kinds of tricks have been tried in the past. Some of the old outfits used to "salt" the water in their box with birdshot just before a muster. When this was pumped out with the water the pellets would carry farther than drops of water. When they hit the paper they hopped away leaving a wet spot.

Some even sneaked and put razor cuts in their opponent's hose. Competition has narrowed down to horizontal water play—and unless some other old hand tub comes along—the record still belongs to Dowagiac—281 feet and 7 inches.

32

Fire Department Organized

Dowagiac's fire department was organized on December 18, 1854 by a group of citizens who wanted some kind of protection of their property. They had had a bad fire in 1853 and lived in dread of another.

Isaiah S. Becraft was chosen as chairman and E.D. Morley, secretary of the meeting. A committee was appointed consisting of R.C. Dennison, Gideon Gibbs and Daniel Lyle "who were authorized to examine the stores, shops and other buildings of the village and ascertain whether proper precautions had been observed by their owners and occupants to guard against the outbreak of fire within them." It recommended that ladders be purchased and held in readiness should an emergency arise.

This was just about all that early fire "department" could do, but early records tell of the purchase of buckets and the building and repairing of cisterns. Rows of cisterns were built along Front Street, and later a reservoir at the corner of Front and Commercial Streets. Each resident dug his own cistern and kept buckets and a ladder handy, each man serving as his own private fire department.

Dowagiac had two bad fires in the 1860's, and the old Union School burning down in the fall of 1859. The rows of wooden store buildings were replaced by brick buildings, most of them still in use today. Some thought the burning of these wooden buildings a blessing, except those merchants who had no insurance. Nine buildings were burned in 1864 and 18 in 1866.

There was another bad fire when nine buildings burned on the east side of Front Street, which was not built up as soon as the west side.

In September, 1885, the Elkerton Hotel, open just a week, burned to the ground. The proprietor promptly rebuilt it identical to the first structure and it opened for business on Christmas Day, 1885. When it was razed a few years ago, Dowagiac's last hotel went out of business. It was located on Park Place beside the railroad and a stone's throw from the depot. That fire started in George Moore's livery stable next door.

It was a mark of prestige for Dowagiac young men to serve with the volunteer fire department. To be a member of a hose or ladder company was a mark of distinction. The fire company members had uniforms and shining and resplendent they would go to dances en masse to dazzle the eyes of the fair sex.

The bad fires of 1885 at the Elkerton Hotel in September and the Round Oak the month following brought things to a head, and after considerable discussion, the city council in December, 1885 voted to buy a steamer, an Amoskeag from Waterford, N.Y. at a cost of $2,000. It came on a Saturday, Feb. 11, 1886.

It was tested out at once and in five mintues after it was fired could produce 10 pounds of steam and in 5½ minutes could throw water. In 10 minutes it could work up to 30 pounds pressure and finally threw a perpendicular stream of water 105 feet through 1,350 feet of hose. But it wasn't good enough and this steamer was sold to Charlevoix, and Dowagiac bought the 6,000 pound Button at $3,750.

Everybody was still sold on steamers even though they watched the slowness of the Amoskeag to be ready for action. The new Button arrived in May, 1886 when Clarence Merwin's ice house caught on fire. The "boys" from the Round Oak Stove Works, who usually had a front seat due to their location downtown, arrived first with their chemical engine which began playing on the flames. The old Cowing hand engine "was soon on the ground and working as usual."

The steamer was on the ground too, "but before a sufficient amount of steam was obtained to make it of any service, the fire was out." The city couldn't see anything but a steamer and a steamer it was until 1912.

But the foresighted P.D. Beckwith wasn't depending on outside sources to protect his stove works, and he provided his factory with ladders, cisterns, buckets, hand extinguishers, and 600 feet or more of hose to go with his hand chemical engine.

New interest was stimulated in the fire department with the arrival of the steamer and a group of young men met on Dec. 11, 1886 and organized themselves into a hose company called "The Alerts." H.E. Larzelere was elected foreman; Arthur Rudolphi, treasurer; Den Onen, secretary; W.C. Edwards, Ed Showerman, George R. Holmes, Fred Blackmond, C.A. Patterson and Clyde Smith making up the rest of the company.

A week later the Hamilton company elected its officers with Mayor Hiram Scovil as president; George Genung, vice president; O.B. Peck, secretary; Talmadge Tice, treasurer; Daniel Rummel, foreman; S.C. Doolittle, first assistant foreman; and Thomas Henwood, second assistant foreman. The old Hamilton Hose company elected E.N. Rogers, foreman; Perry Reynolds, first pipeman; and Ed Pond, second pipemen.

It was voted to take "The Alerts" into the fire department and Thomas Henwood was named fire chief. Each Tuesday night was drill and practice night and regular department meetings held the first and third Thursdays of each month "at 7½ o'clock p.m."

The next important event was the building of the waterworks system in 1887 and installation of water mains and in time, a fire alarm system.

There was still intense rivalry among the companies and the necessity to be there first more important than the fire. The Dowagiac Republican remarked on several occasions, "There seemed to be too many bosses about the fire engine and the handling of the hose to be efficient."

After several more instances the city council in 1888 appointed E. Barlow Jewell its first paid fire chief, which was combined with his office as village marshal. With a "part paid" fire department and his strong hand at the helm, peace reigned.

With the arrival of the new bright red LaFrance fire truck on August 28, 1912, just in time to ride in the Homecoming parade, it marked the end of one era and the beginning of a new motorized age. A company representative spent three days here teaching Harry Scofield how to drive the truck and swing it around the corners.

The old fire department which had held over until the new fire department could take charge, expired. The new fire department, appointed by the city council on August 9, was Dowagiac's first paid fire department. U.P. Leader was held over as fire chief. Lyle Reed was first fireman; Charles Munjoy, second fireman with Harry Scofield as truck driver. Call Firemen were Bert Plummer, Will Stewart, Bert Walters, Art Robison, Ed Brown, and Victor Morse.

The old fire department had voted in July to disband, close up its clubrooms in Firemen's Hall, sell the billiard table and spend whatever money was left on themselves with a banquet.

A few days after the arrival of the fire truck, small boys who couldn't stand the suspense of waiting, turned in a false alarm at the corner of West Railroad and Mechanic Streets. It was estimated that the truck had saved $40 on this false alarm.

The old Button steamer was sold for $50 as junk. When it was dismantled it yielded 946 pounds of copper, 114 pounds of light brass and 85 pounds of yellow brass, "among other things."

33

Fire Stories

A story published in The Daily News concerning one of the bad fires on Front Street, brought denials from a pioneer's daughter, who said it wasn't so. The story came from the late Attorney Don B. ReShore, who had it from his father, Frank ReShore.

He said that during a fire in the 1860's patriotic women had set up a stand and made coffee for the firemen. Also nearby was a keg of whisky and firemen refreshed themselves with both—that is some did. Anyhow it was said that usually sober and staid citizens, some deacons in their church, went home from the fire much the worse for wear.

Another pioneer's daughter, who declined to tell her name, said it was so, because it was her father who set out the keg of whisky. It was cold, bitter weather, she said, and they needed something to warm them besides the exercise.

The old hand pumper afforded much exercise, about 20 men to a side to get the maxium power out of the old tub. The story is told how at one of the fires, Mark Judd manned one side of the pumper, and Mark Oppenheim on the other. Both were short men and when the handle came down on one side, Mark Judd would be lifted off his feet, and when down on the other side, Mark Oppenheim was hoisted into the air.

The new Button steamer did not cover itself with glory in its first test, not due to any deficiency within itself but due to the human element involved. It was a serious matter to The Dowagiac Republican then, but today it sounds amusing.

On a July morning in 1886, the rear portion of William Howser's house was found to be on fire. The Round Oak fire company came with its chemical engine. The old Cowing hand engine was run "to an adjacent cistern and was soon playing on the fire."

The steamer was run to the cistern near the corner of Front and Division and in a short time had steam up and was ready to throw water. For some unaccountable reason the hose carts had been run directly to the fire and the steamer without hose, was impossible to use. All but a small portion of the house burned "though by keeping the flames from the upright the handsome shade trees in front of the house were uninjured. William Hoswer wishes to extend his thanks to all who so faithfully helped at the fire."

Another instance was recorded by The Republican which occured in March, 1885 at the home of Abram Miller on Spruce Street at 2 a.m. Whether firemen and citizens were too sleepy to know what they were doing when they heard the fire bell on the Methodist church, they all hastened to the scene.

"Our citizens responded manfully but they all came barehanded; no engine, no hook or ladder; no hose carts? no thing." So of course there was nothing they could do but let the house burn down. But they did remove the household goods with a minimum of damage.

There was a great fraternal feeling between fire departments and this was particularly true between Dowagiac and Niles. Fire fighting was a welcome break in the daily routine. When Dowagiac was threatened with a fire—what else was there to do but to send a telegram to Niles for help.

Niles was always equal to the job and in a flash would pack an engine, hose carts and practically half the male population "aboard the cars" and be down to Dowagiac in a short time.

The fact the fire was out or the structure had burned down didn't dampen the spirits of either department. The Dowagiac fire department always treated them to supper and a celebration in appreciation of their good intentions.

When the Round Oak machine shop burned out in 1885 the Niles Republican reported: "During the fire at 11:35 a telegram was received in this city from the Mayor of Dowatiac asking for assistance. Before 12o'clock, A.W. Coffinger, chief of our fire department, had an engine, three hose carts, 1,500 feet of hose and 200 men at the Michigan Central depot ready to start for the fire, when Mayor Scovil sent word the fire was under control."

After several of such visits Dowagiac city council voted to make a gift of $100 to the Niles fire department in appreciation for their always willing help and which was acknowledged by both the Niles departmen and Niles city council.

With the steamer, the city fathers decided against buying a team of horses who would be eating their heads off days at a time. Instead they delegated the job to local draymen to haul the engine to the fire. Whoever got there first got paid. Old timers can remember teams racing through the streets, imperilling spectators and themselves in the race to be first.

Firemen were kept busy with drills and hose cart races, and Dowagiac developed a fast running team in the 1880's. Frank Dewey was the lead. It was said that he could run the usual 40 rods or whatever distance was set up, turn after making the required couplings and run back without being winded.

During the 1885 Fourth of July celebration the Hamiltons made the 40-rod run, made a dry coupling in 46 seconds, followed by the Alerts in 46½ seconds.

34

First Fairs

Dowagiac's first fairs were held on the 19th Michigan Infantry campgrounds on the site of the present McKinley School, after the Civil War. The old race track was still visible from the air a few years ago and is still there if there has been no building erected on it.

It was first used to exercise the horses used during the encampment, and then converted into a race track. A grandstand was built and many big races were held here.

This was in no way an agricultural fair, although farm products were exhibited in a small way by the farmers.

In the 1870's the Dowagiac Union Fair was organized and the fairgrounds were moved to the area north of East Division Street, and shown on plat maps as the Fairgrounds Addition.

In the beginning it was a most successful undertaking with buildings and a race track that brought horse race fans from all over. For a time it was Cass County's only fair, the county fair having been discontinued for a time.

Ten thousand people were known to have attended the Dowagiac Union Fair in a day's time. This was also an agricultural fair and there were also many industrial exhibits which made it outstanding.

On fair days the Michigan Central ran special trains to Dowagiac.

Old timers say the ministers and church people "killed off the fair," being opposed to horse racing and betting and a number of other activities that went on there. There were no doubt other reasons, several years of bad weather discouraged attendance, "and caused financial embarassment" it was reported. The grounds were finally sold to satisfy a mortgage which had been placed on the property. By the late 1890's there were no more Dowagiac fairs.

As previously said, Dowagiac's first fairs were primarily horse racing events. Abner Moon reported: "The first Dowagiac fair grew out of the excitement attendant on the racing events which were being held on the west side of the Pokagon pike until recently known as the ball park. (Where Dowagiac baseball games were played in the 1900's).

"William Baldwin, the McCoy boys, Dave Brady, Jeff Gardner and a dozen other old time sport lovers were wont to hold racing events there every week, and finally they chose Sundays for these meets.

"Baldwin (a famous old time auctioneer) was once arrested for thus violating the Sabbath. He knew the warrant was out and kept out of the way of the officers. The warrant was at last given to Peter Youngblood, who laid for Baldwin in his cornfield. When Baldwin saw him coming he exclaimed, 'St. Peter's got me,' and cheerfully accompanied his captor to the justice's office.

"This broke up the Sunday racing but it did not stop the sport lovers from holding races, and the old fairgrounds was born and for a time, flourished."

35

The Beardless Band

One of the predecessors of the famed Round Oak Band was the Dowagiac Silver Cornet band which won itself a reputation all over the countryside nearly a century ago, and this story in The Daily News of Aug. 3, 1909, tell of the "Beardless Band" as it was called.

"That the residents of Dowagiac and vicinity are proud of the Round Oak band and enjoy the Thursday evening concerts is evidenced by the crowds that gather on the street and in the MCRR park every Thursday evening.

"Dowagiac may well feel proud of its band as it has the reputation of being second to none in this part of the state. In fact Dowagiac has for a long time had a spendid musical organization. Even away back in the seventies and sixties the Dowagiac Silver Cornet band had a reputation which could well have been envied by older and larger organizations.

" 'The Beardless Band,' a name given to the Dowagiacs because of the age of its members, was organized in the latter part of the sixties, perhaps in 1863 and consisted originally of 10 pieces, the members being as follows:

"Benjamin Bowling, E cornet; Frank James, B cornet; William Oakley, alto; Spencer McNair, alto; Samuel McCormick, tenor; Herman Bigelow, baritone; Hervey Bigelow, tuba; William Parkison, snare drum; and Darwin Smith, bass drum.

"As is the case with any musical organization it is necessary to take in new recruits. Some will move away, some will retire, while death may cause a vacant place which must be filled.

"Among those who became members later on were: James Russey, E cornet; George Crippen tenor; Ransom Robinson, bass drum; Virgil Harter, B cornet; Otis Bigelow, E cornet; Harmon Defendorf, bass; Rit Van Antwerp, alto; and Millard Swank, B cornet.

"John Rix was the first leader and teacher and he played E cornet. Later on Peter Soules was instructor. The band disbanded in the early eighties but not until they had gained a wide reputation.

"For 11 consecutive years this same beardless band played for the Goodrich Transportation company in Chicago on the 4th of July. A serenade concert was given in the morning before the boats would leave, then it would play aboard boat during the pleasure trips. The steamer, Cheboygan, made four trips from 12 to 14 miles into the lake back and forth each 4th of July, and all but one of the 11 years, the Dowagiac Silver cornet band was on the deck.

"The laying of the corner stone of the old custom house building in Chicago which was recently torn down, was the occasion for a big celebration. The ceremonies were conducted by the Masonic order and each commandery in attendance was accompanied by their own band.

"The parade was divided into four divisions and each dividion was headed by a band hired by the city of Chicago. The Dowagiac band was one of the bands so hired.

"Dowagiac was not yet a city and for a country village band heading a division in a monster parade in the city of Chicago was an honor of which the remaining members speak with much satisfaction.

"The boys played at the State fairs in both Kalamazoo and Jackson, also at the laying of the corner stone of the Michigan state capitol at Lansing."

36

First Orphan Train

In the year 1854 the little village of Dowagiac, still unincorporated, took part in a trail-blazing experiment, in which 47 orphans from New York City were placed in farm homes in this community. In subsequent years thousands of street arabs, abandoned and homeless children were placed in homes all over the mid-west and one of the greatest humanitarian experiments ever conducted in this country.

The American Heritage magazine, a hard-cover magazine published six times a year and one of the country's most prestigious magazines, in its December, 1974 issue, featured "The Children's Migration" by Annette Riley Fry of New York City. This reporter and Mrs. Fry corresponded for two years in an attempt to find descendants of the 47 orphans who came to Dowagiac on the Michigan Central Railroad over 125 years ago. Because the Children's Aid Society in New York City kept skimpy records in the early days and also carefully kept secret the identity of these children, none of their descendants have even been found, with but one exception. And he was not with the first group that came.

He was George Moore, a prominent Dowagiac business man, who came somewhat later in the 1860's, with a brother, believed to be William. Another brother, Charles came later.

Before describing the arrival of the 47 ex-street Arabs, it must be told how this all came about.

Immense numbers of children lived from hand to mouth on New York streets and fast became criminals, prostitutes and vagrants.

They were described as "ragged, verminous, barefoot, the vagrant children slept where they could: in doorways, under stairways, in privies, on hay barges, in discarded packing boxes and on piles of rubbish in alleys and littered back yards."

Mrs. Fry in her lengthy article told in detail how these children were pushed about, authorities saw nothing special about children in those days. In 1830's some children were put in private orphan asylums but this method only took care of a few of them. Charles Loring Brace, a young man just out of the theological seminary, realized the children needed something more and in 1853 organized the Children's Aid Society. It was at a time that New York City with a population of five hundred thousand people, had by police estimates, ten thousand homeless children wandering about the streets. Brace and his colleagues estimated the number as more like 30,000.

So in 1853, Brace, then 26 years old, immediately set to work to do something about these children and issued a circular pointing out their plight and asked to help in establishing industrial schools, lodging houses and reading rooms for the children and for paid agents to care for them, as well as seeking farm homes in the nearby countryside. The response from the homeless waifs themselves was tremendous and who found their way into his office.

Within a month of the time the society was organized Charles Loring Brace placed his first orphan, a 13-year old boy with a family in Woodstock, Conn. It must be remembered these were not foster homes, these homes were given free and the people who took these children cared for them in all respects without recompense.

During that first year children were placed on an individual basis in farm homes in New York, Connecticut and Pennsylvania. It soon became evident that the demand for children from babies to husky teenagers was so great and the number of homeless children in New York City so immense that some other way had to be found to bring adults and children together.

And this is how Dowagiac entered into the picture. Why Dowagiac was selected as the site of the first "orphan train" is not known. This is what Mrs. Fry wrote: "in September, 1854, one of the agents employed by the new society, the Reverend E.P. Smith, chaperoned west the first of the hundreds of groups of emigrant children who were to make the orphan trains almost a part of American folklore.

"The destination of the trailblazing group, boys ranging in age from seven years to fifteen, was the little town of Dowagiac in southwestern Michigan. To reach it they traveled by boat to Albany, by train to Buffalo, by lake boat from Buffalo to Detroit ('with the addition of a touch of seasickness, and of the stamping, neighing and bleating of a hundred horses and sheep over our head,'), and from Detroit to Dowagiac in a car of the Michigan CRR."

A detailed report of the trip from the Children's Aid Society said there were worse things to endure than just the noise, conditions o the boat and train were indescribable.)

"The juvenile emigrants embarked from New York on a Wednesday evening. At 3 a.m. Sunday their train chugged into Dowagiac, where they spent the rest of the night sleeping on the station platform. For most of the forty-six boys (rather forty-seven—in Albany they picked up an urchin with wanderlust) the trip was their first glimpse of the country." The boys are said to have gone down to the Dowagiac Creek on South Front Street and washed as soon as it became daylight.

And this is what the Reverend Mr. Smith wrote: "You can hardly imagine the delight of the children as they looked, many of them for the first time, upon country scenery Each one must see everything we passed, find its name, and make his own comments. 'What's that Mister?" "A cornfield." "Oh. Yes, them's what makes buckwheater." "Look at them cows (oxen plowing) my mother used to milk cows."

Said Mr. Smith, "as we whirled through orchards loaded with large red apples, their enthusiasm rose to the highest pitch. It was difficult to keep them within doors. Arms stretched out, hats swinging, eyes swimming, mouths watering, and all screaming—'oh! oh! just look at 'em! Mister be they any sich in Michigan? Then I am for that place—three cheers for Michigan!"

"We had been riding in comparative quiet for nearly an hour, when all at once the greatest excitement broke out. We were passing a cornfield spread over with ripe, yellow pumpkins. "Oh! younder! look! Just look at 'em!" and in an instant the same exclamation was echoed from forty-seven mouths. "Jist look at 'em!" Ah, fellers, aint that the country tho'—won't we have nice things to eat?" "Yes, and won't we sell some too?" "Hip! hip! boys, three cheers for Michigan!"

"That Sunday morning in the Dowagiac Presbyterian Church, the good people were startled by the presence of the Reverend Smith and his travelworn but still exuberant crew. (Note: There was no Presbyterian Church in Dowagiac—in fact the only church building was the First Baptist Church. However the two-story frame schoolhouse on the site of the former First Methodist Church at Commercial and New York, served as a church on Sundays, and there may have been a Presbyterian Society using it.)

"After the sermon Smith announced the purpose of their visit. And the following day farmers returned to town to put in their applications for boys. By Saturday, all forty-seven had been taken.

The Children's Aid Society kept watch over these children, a job usually delegated to local clergymen, with periodic visits from a representative of the society.

So successful was this first orphan train to Dowagiac, that this custom continued for three-quarters of a century. Agents would find a town interested in receiving orphans, applicants for children would be screened by a committee of local citizens. notices would be placed in newspapers weeks in advance and there was always a crowd on hand to greet the children. Many of the children were adopted into families not only by the childless but by others already with children.

Mrs. Fry has read through many of the reports submitted by agents and found that 90 percent of the orphans made good. Many moved on to other places as they grew up. Among the orphans were two state governors. congressmen, state officials. teachers. clergymen, lawyers, doctors, successful manufacturers, business men, and others who became good citizens.

One of these was the late George W. Moore of Dowagiac. Mrs. Fry corresponded with his grandson, Julius W. Wernicke of Pensacola, Florida, who provided much information about his grandfather. It was first learned that Mr. Moore was a New York orphan some years earlier from his wife. Both he and she were proud of his success and spoke of his early origins freely.

Wernicke mentioned a brother, William coming with George

Moore in the 1860's, and a brother, Charles coming later. However, he may have been mistaken as there seems to be no further mention of William, only of Charles. Their parents came from Ireland and both died in New York City. The Moore boys were not street arabs, but because they had no relatives in this country, were sent to Dowagiac.

George lived with the Miller family in Pokagon Township and Charles with the Andrews family nearby. Mrs. George Moore reported that both worked hard on the respective farms during the week but always had Sunday off. Early Sunday morning the boys would meet each other and spend the day together. Mrs. Moore made no mention of another brother.

She said that George Moore made a vow he would some day own the farm where he lived—and he did. A part of the farm is still owned by his daughter, Maleta Moore Wernicke of Florida. The Moores' two children, Maleta and Charles were both graduates of the University of Michigan. The latter died young at the home of his wife's parents, Mr. and Mrs. Malcolm Campbell in this city.

George Moore worked as a logger, among other jobs, and eventually acquired enough money to build his own store building at the corner of Front and Main Streets where he operated a grocery from 1897 to about 1908 when he sold his grocery stock. The building was sold in 1918 to the late William F. Lyon, for $6,000, the original cost of the building. In the meantime he began building houses in Dowagiac, also a successful project. He was an active member of the Dowagiac Methodist Church.

Mrs. Virgil Rose of Magician Lake and her late husband, Virgil Rose, lived on the Moore farm for years and she cannot say enough about George Moore whom she called "a prince of a fellow."

Information was not available about his brother, Charles, except that he lived here and was also a "solid citizen," and later moved elsewhere in Michigan. His daughter, Viola Moore Hurley was living in Dearborn some years ago.

Of all the orphans who came here only the identity of these two is known.

37

Fourth of July

Dowagiac held its first Fourth of July celebration in 1850. A band came from Elkhart and stayed here two nights. Streets of the little hamlet were crowded. The late Abner Moon described that first celebration:

"Ox teams were the rule, and they came from 20 miles away; came early and stayed late, and it was the happiest gathering ever seen in Dowagiac. Neighbors hitched their teams in convenient woods, visited, ate their dinner together under the shelter of the oaks, listened to the music, the speeches and uproar of the enthusiastic anvil, and watched or took part in the games.

"M.T. Garvey was president of the day, Rev. Justus Gage, the orator, and George B. Turner read the Declaration of Independence, always a religiously kept observance those days, and now never thought of. Dowagiac has had many celebrations since but none that compared with this in its pleasurable features, and today the old residents, say, 'We never had but one Fourth.' "

Dowagiac's next celebration was in 1854, a noisy affair as the others that followed. In 1854 the celebration literally started "with a bang." P.D. Beckwith had come here a few months earlier and was operating his little foundry and repair shop on Park Place Street (as it was known for years) and South Front.

Abram Townsend and several others decided they wanted a loud noisemaker—a cannon and went to Beckwith. He had never made a cannon in all his life but that was a small matter to a man whose name was to go around the world in later years. With limited facilities that would horrify a mechanic of today, he made a cast iron cannon—a good one. It weighed 700 pounds and described as a sleek, streamlined beauty. And he made it for $50. And somehow Abram Townsend was stuck for the whole amount—the rest of the committee had quietly faded away.

This famous cannon was said to have "a voice that caused the wolves of the Newberg hills to seek their dens and echoed across the plains of Jefferson." Eager as small boys, this group of grown men took their prize out to the South Park (where City Hall stands) and when it came dawn the cannon gave out its initial roar.

That first blast broke the windows in the rooms over the Gibbs and Townsend store across the way which were then occupied by Mr. and Mrs. Francis Mosher. Then they moved it to the north park. It was placed on a knoll under an old oak tree. The firing kept up until the gun grew hot, and the man "thumbing the vent" had to let go. The premature discharge cost Sam Benson his left hand, but that failed to stop the enthusiastic celebrators. The firing kept up until dark.

The cannon did faithful duty at every celebration in Dowagiac for years, anywhere noise was desired. One Fourth of July when a stone was placed in the old cannon, then in the south park, it was propelled with such force that it went through the wooden front of a store building on Beeson Street. The stone was left there and the hole pointed out for years.

The old cannon finally gave up the ghost some time before the turn of the century and Abner Moon described how it happened. "It happened about 5:45 a.m. Messrs. Henry Savage and Will Alliger reared the old cannon on end and inserted four sticks or two pounds of dynamite, and touched it off.

"The explosion was heard for miles, and the shower of fragments of the cannon was felt more than a quarter of a mile away in every direction, but fortunately no one was hurt.

"A fragment weighing about ten pounds descended upon the Robert Watson residence on East High Street, and passed completely through the roof, smashing a sewing machine stand and wash bowl as it went. Another fragment struck a glancing blow on the side of the Fred Lewis residence on Park Place Street. Another damaged the edge of the roof at the Michael Herold residence on Main Street, another at the corner of Front and Commercial, another struck the Beckwith photograph studio."

It was left (what remained of it) to rust away in the weeds near the Judd Lumber Company and the late Mark Judd was always intending to have a hitching post made out of its remains, but he never got around to it.

38

The Dowagiac Diamond

Isaac Wells Sr., who found Michigan's only diamond near Cook Lake north of Dowagiac in June, 1894 -- an off white diamond weighing slightly over 11 carats. Since then, every time the story is printed, diamond hunters invade this area hoping to find its mate. The May-June, 1976 issue of "Michigan Natural Resources" magazine is the latest to revive interest. Reader's Digest, Saturday Evening Post and other periodicals have in years past written about this one lone diamond produced in Michigan.

But before bringing up to date and repeating the story and the whereabouts of the diamond, here is something about the man who found it. A resident of Dowagiac for many years, Isaac Wells Sr. was born in Greene County, Ohio, and in October, 1831, came to Edwardsburg with his parents, Mr. and Mrs. Charles Wells.

A few years later they moved to Bertrand Township, Berrien County, they being one of the first five families who settled on the old "Indian Reserve," at that time inhabited by a band of some 480 Potawatomi Indians. His childhood days were spent with the few white children and the numerous Indian boys who lived on the old Reserve. He learned to speak the Potawatomi language fluently and could speak it all of his life and was always on the most friendly terms with the Indians. He often served as an interpreter for the Indians and made trips to Tippecanoe on the Kankakee with Topinabee on hunting and fishing expeditions. according to a story written about him at the time of his death in 1912 in his home on Main Street.

He learned blacksmithing from his older brothers and continued this trade into the 1850's, shoeing many horses, mules and oxen that made the trip to California in the gold rush days. He used to tell how he would stay up until all hours of the night making nails from crude iron for use of the following day.

After his marriage to Sarah J. Herkimer of Bertrand Township in 1857 they moved to Cass County where he engaged in farming. In 1880 they moved to Dowagiac. He became a contractor in sand and **gravel for the Round Oak Company. Mrs. Clarence Gillette of Niles is a granddaughter, John Gillette, of Berrien Springs, president of the Michigan Historical Society.**

After his marriage to Sarah J. Herkimer of Bertrand Township in 1857 they moved to Cass County where he engaged in farming. In 1880 they moved to Dowagiac. He became a contractor in sand and gravel for the Round Oak Company. Mrs. Clarence Gillette of Niles is a granddaughter, John Gillette, of Berrien Springs is a great-grandson.

The gravel pit, located on land now owned by the Dowagiac Conservation Club was where Isaac Wells was loading gravel one day when he caught sight of a stone that sparkled and looked much different from the others.

He took the stone to Fred Blackmond, a young Dowagiac jeweler who was pretty sure it was a diamond. Fred Blackmond was a grandson of Wells' old time friend, Nicholas Bock, who died in 1885. Both were early pioneers here. Blackmond sent the stone to the Curator of Minerals at the Smithsonian Institution in Washing, where it was pronounced a diamond. Tiffany's the New York jewelers, also appraised it but nobody knows what its value was rated at that time as Tiffany records back for those years are gone.

Fred Blackmond bought the diamon of Wells for $100, and according to Esther Middlewood, it was to be kept secret until after Wells' death, it being presumed he didn't want other people searching the gravel pit. Wells, it is said, did search for other possible diamonds but none were ever found. It is presumed it was a "loner" swept down from a hidden nest of still undiscovered diamonds somewhere up in Canada. When the location was finally learned, the gravel pit had filled with water, the condition it is still in today.

Blackmond, it is said, decided to have a professional diamond cutter cut up the stones which he wanted made into rings. The firm of Stein and Ellbogen Company of Chicago did the work, and much of the original diamond was lost as waste, but four stones, each containing about one carat each were made into rings which were given to family members. Later two stones were made into one ring which Steve Blackmond of Logansport, Ind., formerly of Dowagiac, a grandson of Fred Blackmond, now owns, and the other two rings belongs to his sister, Kathryn, Mrs. Gil Lenning of Steubenville, Ohio.

39

The Civil War

Up until World War I -- "The War" was the Civil War in Dowagiac and probably most everywhere else. The Spanish-American War, sandwiched in between these two wars, was largely ignored.

As a child I remember old gray-haired men, standing down town on street corners, still fighting Civil War battles. They were always referred to as "the old soldiers," or "the boys in blue." If his name appeared in a local newspaper usually some reference was made to his war service. I can remember several living in my neighborhood. On Memorial Day, called Decoration Day then, out came as much of their old uniforms as they could muster up, and especially their hats, and they marched or rode in the annual parade.

It has been said that Cass County sent almost as many men to fight in the Civil War as it did in World War II. This hardly seems probable although the proportion of men serving in the Civil War was higher due to a much smaller population in the county in those days.

Cass County histories list these veterans by names and regiments, reporting a total of 1,675 men as serving.

One Civil War regiment, the 19th Michigan Infantry, and three Civil War companies were organized in Dowagiac, starting with the Cass County Guards which later became Company E of the 42nd Illinois Regiment; followed by Company D of the Sixth Michigan Infantry; Company M of the First Michigan Cavalry; and the 19th Michigan Infantry Regiment.

Many from Dowagiac had enlisted in the 12th Michigan Infantry at Niles. Company A was recruited at Cassopolis. John Gillette, publisher of Hardscrabble Books, and a former president of the Historical Society of Michigan, has done considerable research on the 12th Michigan Infantry.

This particular story will deal with the 19th Michigan Infantry Regiment. Early historians have remarked that there were fewer Dowagiac men in the 19th Michigan Infantry due to the fact it was not recruited until the summer of 1862.

Although the 19th Michigan was Dowagiac's own regiment, it will not be covered as deeply as it otherwise would. Dr. William Anderson, president of Carl Sandburg College at Galesburg, Illinois, has done an outstanding and detailed history of the regiment in his book, published in December, 1980, "They Died to Make Men Free."

Dr. Anderson, an early staff member of Southwestern Michigan College near Dowagiac, became interested in the regiment while living here. He also did some researching on Company E of the 42nd Illinois, which is another story. The tremendous amount of research he did makes this an unusually interesting book.

This is a part of what he had to say about his book in his introduction: "Despite many similarities, each Civil War regiment was different, its unique cast of characters accounted for much of the difference. This is a story of a group of civilians (about a thousand or so) who agreed to help fight a war . . . no question, the Civil War was the central experience in their lives."

He goes on to say: "This then, is a history retold by the participants, where the major contributors are officers and enlisted men who wrote letters to families and friends and to home town newspapers, and conscientiously recorded entries in personal diaries and journals. In all, the author has become aware of 823 letters written by 16 officers and 33 enlisted members of the 19th Michigan Infantry Regiment.

"Additionally, the recollections of 10 members were preserved in diaries and journals. Among the letters, almost 90 percent were written by enlisted men . . . and eight local newspapers had 'correspondents' within the regiment, one of them being a former editor. Some of these knew they were writing for publication but most wrote privately and personally, often instructing wives to keep the contents confidential."

Dr. Anderson said: "One gets to know Sergeant Phineas Hager after reading and studying 84 letters to his wife, the first written the day his company arrived at the rendezvous camp (Dowagiac) in August, 1862, and the last just days before his life was claimed by a sniper's bullet before Atlanta in August, 1864 . . . Thus when Sergeant Hager died on August 8, 1864, Sherman lost a top-notch veteran and I lost his discerning eyes and descriptive pen."

Particularly interesting is how the 19th Michigan practically rebuilt McMinniville, Tenn. where the regiment was stationed for several months. Dowagiac was selected because it was the center of the congressional district at that time and on the Michigan Central Railroad.

Dr. Anderson had some assistance from Robert Schultz of St. Joseph, formerly of Dowagiac, and a 19th Michigan Infantry "buff," who on vacation trips, used to follow the 19th Michigan's line of march during the war. Schultz reported that the total enrollment of the regiment was 1,206. Of this number 54 were killed in action; 31 died of their wounds; 7 died in Confederate prisons; 132 died of disease; and 182 were discharged for disability.

The best description of the 19th Michigan Infantry campgrounds located near the railroad and occupying the site of the present McKinley School and adjacent territory, was given by the late Flavia Defendorf of Dowagiac.

She was 15 years old when the Civil War broke out, and she remembered the barracks built on the campgrounds. There was no viaduct over the railroad then. On Sunday it was the custom of the townspeople to drive to the camp in their horse-drawn carriages, and watch the soldiers drill. The camp was surrounded by a high board fence.

The basket factory was commandeered as an army hospital and usually pretty well occupied. The young soldiers were not neglected, women of the community were constantly taking chicken broth and other food thought suitable for the sick and the men never lacked for attention. The people of Dowagiac were intensely patriotic and did what they could to make camp life as bearable as possible, for no doubt there was many a case of homesickness after the first excitement had worn off. One soldier died in this hospital.

Girls of the community were most happy to have these young men in town and how many romances flourished, at this late date will never be known.

While the 19th was still here, two boys of the town, Frank Jones, father of the late Lisle and Walter Jones, and Sanford Smith, whose father was Captain Joel Smith of Company A, bought a load of watermelons and took them to the campgrounds to sell. The boys, still in their teens, were mobbed and the melons confiscated.

When the boys demanded pay for them, the soldiers just laughed. But the laugh was soon on them when they realized the Smith boy's father was Captain Smith. A hat was passed and the boys received double the amount the melons were worth.

The day the boys were to leave for the war was well known in advance and hundreds of people for miles around flocked to the little village to "bid the boys goodbye and wish them a safe return." In response to the tremendous reception some of the soldiers made speeches. Among them was Reason Davis, to be well known in later years as the evangelist, "Stormy" Davis.

A witness to this occasion said that though Davis was "a rough, uneducated man of the world, his soul was afire with patriotism and the words he spoke that day brought tears to the eyes of many and are often recalled by those who heard them."

After the soldiers left, their training grounds were turned into a fairgrounds. An aerial view taken of Dowagiac some years ago showed the circle where horses used at the camp were exercised and which later became a race track. And if this spot has not been built over, even though well over a century ago, this track is still there.

There was a long building near the railroad track where women of the First Baptist Church, and possibly others, sold food and other items to raise funds for the Sanitary Commission, the organization which preveded the Red Cross. They started doing this while the 19th Michigan was still in training there, and how much longer is not known.

40

Organized in Dowagiac

Besides Company E of the 42nd Illinois regiment, there were two other companies organized in Dowagiac. Company D of the Sixth Michigan Infantry was organized in Dowagiac in the summer of 1861, the regiment being rendezvoused at Kalamazoo, and was sent to Detroit for two months of training. It was the first regiment to occupy New Orleans. It took part in many engagements in Louisiana. A third of the regiment's men were killed at Port Hudson including men from Cass County.

Uzziel Putnam Jr. of Pokagon Township, the first white child born in Cass County, served with Company D as a private and was discharged for disability in 1864.

Company M of the First Michigan Cavalry was from Cass County, and other Cass County men were scattered through other companies of the regiment. It was mustered into service on September, 18, 1861 and spent several months at Camp Frederick, Md. near Washington, D.C. Its battles were all in Virginia. After a winter of guard duty in front of Washington, the First was assigned to the Michigan Cavalry Brigade of which General George Custer was commander. The First went to Fort Bridger, Utah with Custer.

A number from Dowagiac served with Company A of the 12th Michigan Infantry which rendezvoused at Niles.

41

Company E

The story of Company E of the 42nd Illinois Infantry Regiment is an interesting one. This company was organized in Dowagiac in April, 1861 as the Cass County Guards.

Many local people have stored away, the Civil War Diary of James Riley of Volinia Township, which was published in The Dowagiac Daily News in serial form in the 1960's. The diary was loaned by his granddaughter, Pauline Goodenough. Riley became famous in later years as a spiritualist medium and was visited by hundreds through the years. Mrs. Goodenough lived next door to her grandfather when she was a child.

After remaining in barracks in Dowagiac for six weeks, this company was assigned to the Fourth Michigan Volunteer Infantry Regiment at Adrian. It was subsequently assigned to the Sixth and then ordered dispersed because the men refused to go to Detroit for further training. The company voted unanimously to offer themselves for reenlistment in the Douglas Brigade then forming in Chicago, and were accepted. On July 26, 1861, these 62 men were mustered in at Dowagiac as Company E, of the 42nd Illinois Volunteer Infantry, by Capt. Webb, U.S. mustering officer, according to records of the Adjutant General's office of Illinois.

The 42nd moved around Missouri, Tennessee, Mississippi, Alabama, and the siege of Atlanta. They reenlisted and after the war the regiment was sent to Fort Bridger, Utah, and was finally mustered out in 1866.

Not all went including James Riley, who fought all through the war, and who spent his boyhood among the Potawatomi Indians and was not about to go out to Utah and fight Indians.

Fortunately Mrs. Goodenough has recorded how her grandfather's regiment was on board ship on the Mississippi River, headed for Utah. Riley jumped ship and swam to shore amidst a hail of bullets. He had a rough time making his way home. It was some years before he could obtain his honorable discharge.

Joseph L. Sturr, a son of Jacob Sturr, a pioneer resident of Dowagiac, who spent his boyhood in Dowagiac, was living in Decatur in 1916 when he told of his experiences with Company E.

"Mr. Sturr says that himself, John Hoover, Jim Riley (the medium), George Spicer, Lucian Day, Ashur Huff, William Codding, George Higgins, John Neville, Jehial Hall and William Colburn -- all familiar names here -- served together throughout the war. They enlisted in what was known as the Cass County Guards, although Cass County did not then need any guards. The organizers were Dan McOmber, captain and William Townsend and Nat Defoe, lieutenants -- all dead.

"Failing to get admission in a Michigan regiment they went to Illinois and finally became a part of the Douglas Brigade, afterward the Forty-second Illinois Infantry. A new election of officers resulted in another being named captain of the company and Mr. McOmber came home.

(After being sworn in at Dowagiac and going to Chicago, McOmber came home to attend to some business affairs -- and it was while he was gone that he lost his job as captain.)

"Jim Riley was a good soldier," said Mr. Sturr. "Lieutenant Townsend often afflicted Jim and I and we often plotted to get even with him when opportunity came. After the Stone River battle Jim told me that during a charge Townsend was ahead of him. He saw his chance to even up and sighted his gun on Townsend, but relented and turned his weapon on the enemy." (Riley related this incident in his diary.)

"With the exception of Hall (Jehial Hall who was killed in action) we all returned home after the war without a wound and but a little worse in a way for our long service.

"After the battle of Lookout Mountain we had nothing to do

except explore the country and many of us secured a cane for a relic. I lost mine soon after."

Robert Gill Burling was another Dowagiac man who served with Company E of the 42nd Illinois Infantry. He not only served with Company E, but after recovering from a disability, enlisted with Company A of the 19th Michigan Infantry and served until the end of the war. He was wounded at Averysboro, N.C. on March 16, 1865. He died here in 1901 and is buried in the little private cemetery on Pokagon Street known as the Hamilton-Burling Cemetery.

42

Dead Man's Hollow

The story of Dead Man's Hollow gives some idea of the division of feelings about the Civil War -- not all Dowagiac residents were northern sympathizers.

What really happened can easily be verified today as the original papers from the inquest are still intact and on file in the offices of County Clerk Kenneth M. Poe in Cassopolis.

Dead Man's Hollow is located on M-62 East in Section 9 of LaGrange Township. The "hollow" lies between the Chester Ball and Charles K. Price Jr.'s places and is crossed by the Dowagiac Creek.

In August, 1863, the Civil War was a war pretty close to home and it didn't take much to rouse people almost to the point of hysteria, especially when a man was killed and that man was John Letts, a U.S. deputy provost marshal.

The Knights of the Golden Circle had been organized for the alleged purpose of rescuing rebel prisoners confined at Fort Douglas in Chicago. A local order had been established in Dowagiac, so they said, and it was also alleged that arms and ammunition had been received and were at the Dowagiac depot at the time of the killing of Letts.

Many local citizens were expecting an uprising among the copperheads or southern sympathizers, so when they heard of Letts' death, they barricaded their houses and the town was picketed.

John Letts lived in a house at the corner of North Front and Merchant Street, which formerly belonged to the late Mrs. George

Bennett and recently razed. The Asa Huntington family lived on the other corner, site of Holy Maternity Catholic Church. Their daughter, Flavia Defendorf, then a young girl, remembered the night when John Letts' body was brought home.

I am going to let Abner Moon, an early historian and newspaper man, take it from here.

"About a mile northwest of LaGrange the Dowagiac Creek crosses the wagon road near the home of Mr. A. Secor. The woods upon the southwest side of the road at that time contained the old growth of mammoth oak. On the opposite side of the road, the same kind of timber prevailed. This was a dark place even on moonlight nights, as the road was narrow, and the old patriarch oaks arched thickly over the highway. Some work had been done on the road, consisting principally of cutting down the grade just wide enough for teams to pass. In this cut, some few rods west of the bridge, which at that time stood close to the south bank of the road, the tragedy herein related took place.

"There lived at that time in Dowagiac a man abut 45 years of age, who kept a livery stable where Hubbard's barn now stands. (On Pennsylvania Avenue on the site of the Amersdorfer & Wiltse Insurance Agency). His name was John Letts. Mr. Letts had secured the appointment of Deputy United States marshal for this district, and also acted as provost marshal, an office especially relating to the war. He spent most of his time running down deserters from the army.

"On the fatal evening Marshal Letts, behind his span of black roadsters, drove up to Hank Martin's saloon, which stood about where George Rapp's place is now located. (This was at 101 Front Street in 1899). He went inside, ordered drinks, bought a bottle of whiskey, and running his eyes over the setters in the place, discovered one Bob Campbell, the wayward brother of William Campbell, then postmaster of Dowagiac and editor of one newspaper, The Dowagiac Republican.

"Bob wasn't married, at least to anything visible except 'Old Budge'. He was a man about 25 years old, above average stature, good natured, and apparently had no desire to injure any human being other than himself. He was pretty groggy at the time and appeared to the United States Marshal to be a suitable companion for a trip toward the southeast part of the county, he had started to make that night. "Come Bob, you must go with me tonight," were the well remembered words of the marshal, and both men climbed into the buggy and were off by way of LaGrange.

"On this day an old-fashioned gang of threshers were separating the wheat from the chaff and straw at Norman Jarvis's farm (now part of the campus of Southwestern Michigan College) where the brick house now stands on McKinney's prairie. Among the persons at that threshing were William Simpson, William Crowell and their wives. Mr. Simpson and Mrs. Crowell were brother and sister, and Mrs. Norman Jarvis, also Mrs. Zed Jarvis were sisters of Mr. Simpson and Mrs. Crowell. Mr. Simpson lived where Anthony Secor now lives, near the bridge, and Mr. Crowell lived on the east and west road on the north side of the LaGrange millpond. (Lake LaGrange).

"About dark, Simpson and Crowell and their wives, left the Jarvis farm with a load of wheat, coming this way to the Bucklin corner, then turning toward their homes and the fatal 'Dead Man's Hollow.'

"They were hardly well straightened into that road, leading past Abram Fiero's, when the marshal and his companion -- both pretty hilarious -- came driving up behind. It is reported that Marshal Letts let loose some epithets very uncomplimentary to the ladies, as likewise to the men, and ordered the team out of the road.

"They not turning out, Letts wheeled out, went by them, dallied along in front in an attempt to impede the progress of the farmers, hoping to witness a vain effort on their part to drive past him.

"It seems this kept up more or unless until the cut in the road by the hollow was reached, when the marshal and his companion stopped, blocking the road and waiting for the farmer team.

"Two things were quite evident: First that the Martin whiskey was a belligerent brand; second that Mr. Letts was not aware who was in the farmer's wagon. While William Simpson was an upright, law-abiding, peaceful citizen, respected in his community, he wore one of those firm chins that project down and outward, which when properly read, plainly notified all intruders of inalienable rights, that they are treading on dangerous ground. Mr. Simpson was not quite so tall nor so heavy as Mr. Letts, but more resolute and determined in action when put upon.

"It is reasonable to suppose that by this time Mr. Simpson's 'blood was getting up,' as the saying goes. On driving up Mr. Letts was asked to move to one side of the road sufficient to let the load of wheat pass by but the response was overbearing and insulting, as reported by the farmers and their wives, when Simpson jumped from his wagon took the bits of Letts's team and began to move the rig enough to the side of the road to let Crowell drive through.

"This act incensed Letts who couldn't quite understand how ordinary people would dare to exercise such rights when the deputy United States marshal was at the other end of the performance, so he jumped from his buggy, rushed toward Simpson, revolver in hand and snapped the same, which failed to go off, apparently as a mercy to justice and both parties engaged.

"Right here, Bob Campbell, who sat in the buggy, if he had been sober enough, might have taken his first cognizance of the kind of material Farmer Simpson was made of. Quicker than a flash Simpson planted his fist so hard against the side of Letts's head that he Letts went down like a ten-year old boy.

"Simpson moved the team and Crowell drove through and they with their wives went to their respective homes leaving Campbell to revive the marshal. Now comes the ludicrous part of the narrative. After quite a time Campbell got it through his groggy head that his boss had ceased to breathe. Then came visions, not of snakes, but of secessionists, rebels, copperheads, all armed with rifles, bayonets and swords, and to avoid further conflict with so deadly a class of men, Bob concluded to avoid the highway and get home by the shortest route.

"He drove into the woods and down through the swales, then up and across the Abram Fiero farm and so in a nearly straight line for town, coming in breathless and hatless, reporting that Letts and himself had been attacked by a brigade or at least a whole company of rebels, that the marshal was killed and only by the shrewdest sagacity of mind and the fleetness of a pair of legs did he manage to come out of the first Civil War skirmish in Michigan. He was sure that there were at least 30 of the attacking party and they carried bayonets for he saw them. It was true that two 3-tined pitchforks were in the wagon, sticking, handle ends down, between the bags and box, the tines being up in the air.

"Of course excitement was rife upon our streets; and every good citizen was up in arms -- mentally at least. But a few wiser ones, who knew Bob, drove out there, stopping at Abram Fiero's, engaging him and his team to assist and brought in the body.

"The following day reports of the killing spread with lightning rapidity, reaching of course the ears of William Simpson, who for the first time suspicioned that he was the cause of the death of the marshal. Simpson at once drove to town, recited the events of the night before, and gave himself up to the officers of the law.

"A coroner's jury of six men was impaneled, the body carried to a spot just south of the freight house, where the jury listened to the sworn statements of Bob Campbell, Mr. and Mrs. Crowell and Mr. and Mrs. Simpson. Campbell's statement was rambling and inconsistent in the main, a part of it being contradictory and impossible. The jury brought in a verdict of justifiable homicide."

43

Civil War Incidents

The Dowagiac Daily Union was born of the Civil War and three issues of this less than tabloid size newspaper are still in existence today. It was published in the Republican office by William H. Campbell. The issue of April 23, 1861 reported that Cass County was aroused:

"After a very brief notice a large and enthusiastic Union meeting, without distinction of party, was held at Larzelere's Hall, on Thursday evening last. Speeches were made by S.N. Gantt, James M. Spencer and others, after which a paper was circulated and about thirty young men enrolled themselves as members of the first Company of volunteers from this village. The meeting then adjourned to meet at the Wigwam on Friday evening the Hall not being large enough or strong enough to hold the crowd.

"On Friday afternoon, a beautiful Union pole, of ash and hickory, was raised on the public square, amid the most intense and heartfelt enthusiasm ever manifested by our citizens, and when our glorious stars and stripes were run up, cheer upon cheer were given with the wildest demonstrations of joy.

"In the evening another large meeting was held in the Wigwam, which was addressed by G.C. Jones, R.C. Denison, S.N. Gantt, James Sullivan and Joseph B. Clarke. The speeches were able and patriotic, and the eloquent words met a ready response from the people.

"After the speeches the Dowagiac Glee Club, who were present, came forward and sang several patriotic songs, including "The Star

Spangled Banner" by Mr. Deyo, assisted by the entire assemblage. Mr. Defendorf's Martial Band then favored the meeting with several patriotic airs and the meeting adjourned. During the whole proceedings, the enthusiasm and spirit was really intense. The frequent loud applause and volumes of cheers attested the heartfelt approval with which the words of the speakers were met.

"Cass County will do her whole duty in this great emergency, and her sons will be heard from wherever the voice of duty calls. At the close of the meeting the enlistment roll was again presented and some twenty more young men joined the Company to serve their country and protect its flag.

"On Saturday evening a large meeting was held at Cassopolis, the Court House we understand, being crowded to its fullest extent. Patriotic but brief remarks were made by A.J. Smith, Charles W. Clisbee and others, and eight more recruits joined the Company. The Company, we understand, is now full, and are ready and exceedingly anxious of being called into active service.

"The young men comprising this organization are worthy of all encouragement and praise for their patriotic determination to volunteer in the National defense; and it is to be hoped that our citizens will contribute of their means all sums that shall be necessary to place this Volunteer organization in the highest state of efficiency for actual service."

This was how the Cass County Guards, later Company E of the 42nd Illinois came into being.

General Burnside Here

Mrs. Flavia Defendorf recalled that in the spring of 1863 General Burnside paid an unexpected visit to Dowagiac and purely by accident. He had been to Chicago to suppress a newspaper, The Chicago Times, published by a southern sympathizer, Wilbur F. Story. Close to Dowagiac his train had some sort of breakdown and General Burnside and his party came here.

Mrs. Defendorf said the fire bell on top of the Methodist Church was rung and the whole town turned out for a public demonstration, and General Burnside was prevailed upon to make a speech. He later became commander-in-chief of the Union armies.

Another big demonstration occurred when word was received from Kalamazoo that Vicksburg had fallen. Soon the whole village was fired up with excitement for Vicksburg had been considered the stronghold of the whole Confederacy and with its surrender would come the end of the war.

A monster bonfire was made that night. Dry goods boxes, timber and anything obtainable and burnable was carted to the park. Bells were rung, war songs were sung and speeches made by prominent citizens. As far as Dowagiac was concerned -- the war was over.

Another minor incident during the war occurred, showing that there were southern sympathizers or "copperheads" as they were sometimes called, in the community. Some of the boys had made an image of Jefferson Davis and left it hanging by the neck from an old tree in the 500 block of Green Street.

Some of the farmers who were southern sympathizers coming into town, saw it and proceeded to pull it down. They were greeted by a volley of clubs and stones from the boys which made them change their minds. "It was a victory for the boys for which they received the plaudits of the village," according to an old Daily News story.

The Civil War didn't come as a "bolt out of the blue." It had been building up for some time and there were strong feelings in this northern community. James. L. Gantt who had established the Dowagiac Tribune here in 1854 began showing a slant toward the south and this did not sit well with many local residents. They tried to persuade him to mend his ways but he refused.

"The boys, according to an early reporter, "Many of whom wore beards, hauled an old cast iron cannon to his residence (site of the present post office) and fired it beneath his bedroom window. The warning was sufficient. The Tribune ceased to issue and the Gantts left town."

This is not exactly the true ending. After complaining loudly through his newspaper, Gantt sold out to W.H. Campbell, publisher of The Republican. This was about the year 1859.

44

Custer

For a few years after the Civil War Dowagiac residents were thrilled by visits from the famous war general, General George Armstrong Custer -- just how many is not known. It is known he came in 1868 and some say in the spring of 1876, the year he lost his life in the west.

There were at least two reasons he came -- one is that Mrs. Custer, formerly Elizabeth Bacon, was a relative of the Walter G. (Dick) Beckwith family, then living in Dowagiac. The other reason is that before the Civil War Custer was a breeder of good horses at his farm near Monroe in this state.

At the time of the Custers' visits here, Beckwith operated a boot and shoe shop in Dowagiac. Before the Custers went west, he made a pair of high stoga boots for Mrs. Custer.

Beckwith was president of the Michigan Fair Association and member of the state agricultural board and prominently known throughout the state. He owned an 800-acre farm in Jefferson Township where much of his life was spent. Whenever speakers of national fame came to Cass County he was always delegated to meet them and escort them, one of them being Daniel Webster. Beckwith shared an interest in horses and horse racing with General Custer and this was a strong reason for the latter coming to see him.

Company M of the First Michigan Cavalry was recruited at Dowagiac and most of its original members came from Dowagiac and Cass County. The First Michigan Cavalry during the war became a part of Custer's Brigade. Among those still with Company M included John Bilderback, Halbert Taylor of Dowagiac and Clark Beardslee of Marcellus.

In 1868 when General and Mrs. Custer came to Dowagiac, the general inquired if any of his "boys" lived here. Beckwith knew that Edward Henwood had served with a New York regiment which was part of the Custer Brigade. Beckwith sent for him where he was working.

Somewhere I had the date of this old Dowagiac Republican story and which was later repeated in The Dowagiac Daily News some years later, but it has become lost. It was probably written by Julius O. Becraft, the Republican owner and editor.

"After washing up and donning his soldier clothes, Edward Henwood pinned on his regimental badge and came to the store. For two hours he and the great general visited and talked over the days of battle, of the beautiful Shenandoah Valley which Custer's troops had devastated in his successful fight to subdue the stubborn southerners, and their later campaigns in the west."

After Lee's surrender in 1865 Henwood's regiment took part in the grand review of the soldiers at Washington before General Grant. General Custer had bought for every one of his boys a handsome red scarf, and each wore this in the parade. They received much praise as they rode down Pennsylvania Avenue on their horses which also had been prepared for the occasion.

When Edward Henwood went to see General Custer "he wore the scarf he had on at the grand review in Washington and their visit was one of the brightest two hours in his life."

Henwood's regiment was ordered west with Custer. In June 1866 he was discharged at Fort Bridger, Utah.

In subsequent visits both John Bilderback and Halbert Taylor had a chance to visit with General Custer. "Custer's striking figure, his long hair and handsome features made him a personage never forgotten by those who saw him in those days."

"There were six Henwood brothers, Edward, Will, Richard, Thomas, James and John. Their parents came from England to Canada. They came to Dowagiac from Canada. Thomas came first and was employed by Daniel Lyle. Edward went to work for P.D. Beckwith, until he sold out his shop on South Front Street to Enos and Guy Chappell. He remained with the Chappells for three years, then returned to Beckwith's employ."

Company M of General George Custer's First Michigan Cavalry was given gredit by General Custer in his book, "Michigan in the War," for saving the day on the third day of the fight at Gettysburg. Of the 102 Cass County men who served with the First Michigan Cavalry, 75 were with Company M. Altogether there were 54 men in the First Michigan from Dowagiac, and 32 of the 75 in Company M were from Dowagiac. Company M was recruited in Dowagiac in 1861.

Local histories carefully avoid any reference to the pressure put upon men to stay in the army, after the war was over, and go west with Custer to fight the Indians. They could not legally be made to go, they had enlisted to fight "for the duration," and many had reenlisted at the end of their three years' service and had served over four years.

When these men did go west and fight the Indians, they were treated shamefully. They were discharged at Ft. Bridger, Utah, and then abandoned. They were forced to pay their own way home or walk.

Among the Cass County men who went west were Mathew B. Dopp, John W. Robinson, Charles Meacham, Isaac DeWitt, Andrew J. Ellsworth and James P. Wiley of Dowagiac; Halbert E. Taylor and Philip Angle of Wayne Township; Richard L. Crawford, Penn; Wesley C. Randall, Jefferson; First Lieut. John Munson, Joseph Morlan, John Grush and Lewis James of Volinia and George Krupp of Pokagon.

Joseph D. Morlan of Volinia Township said that the cavalrymen were dressed warmer than the men who marched on foot. Besides woolen suits they were outfitted with long overcoats with capes and carried a saber, repeating carbine and pistol.

They also carried their own supplies, hardtack, corn and most always edible roots in their saddlebags, a blanket roll, and if lucky, an extra suit of underwear and socks, a canteen, mostly made of wood or tin, and a tin cup. Morlan was a good cook and often did his own cooking as many did.

He reenlisted in January, 1864 and the company returned to

Michigan for a 30-day furlough. From Kalamazoo they left for St. Louis and waited two months for horses, arms and equipment. They went south and drove Rebel General Shelby beyond the Arkansas River and dispersed bands of guerrillas. This time the regiment was armed with the new Spencer repeating carbine. They were stationed at Brownsville, Texas, and moved up through Mississippi and Tennesse marching almost 1,000 miles.

At the time The First Michigan went west to fight hostile Indians there were about 170,000 whites scattered through the west and 90 percent of them were males. It was said the soldiers' "companions" were the buffalo, wild horses, jack rabbits and coyotes.

"Trouble was constantly brewing and there was brutality on both sides, history says. The Indians clung to their old hunting grounds and were finally killed off in such great numbers that those remaining had to flee for their lives."

45

The Clarke Brothers

There were six Clarke brothers, natives of Lebanon, Conn., three of whom lived in Dowagiac. One was Colonel Charles E. Clarke who was commissioned captain of Company D, of the Sixth Michigan Infantry, recruited in Dowagiac. Another brother, Dr. William Clarke, who practiced medicine here before the Civil War, served as an army surgeon, leaving Dowagiac for Chicago after the war. The other brother who lived here was Attorney Joseph B. Clarke, whose home was at 206 Green St.

Joseph Clarke's son, First Lieutenant (acting Captain) Frederick J. Clarke, also served with Company D. He was killed while leading his company in a desperate assault upon a portion of the rebel fortification of Port Hudson, La., on May 27, 1863. His body was recovered from under the continued rebel fire, by his uncle, assisted by the drummer boy of the regiment and two colored soldiers, and removed to and buried in the National Military Cemetry at Baton Rouge.

Through successive promotions Charles Clarke became colonel. He served with the regiment under Generals Butler and Banks; commanded the principal part of his regiment in the successful battle of Baton Rouge, though then only a captain, the regiment's officers being absent in New Orleans, and was in command of Fort Morgan, Mobile Bay after its capture. After being mustered out at Jackson in 1865 he reenlisted in the regular army with the rank of major, serving until 1880.

In the late 1830's and early 1840's Frederick Clarke, another brother of Attorney Joseph Clarke, and who spent considerable time in Dowagiac, was one of the best known men along the Ohio River. During the Civil War he served as commissary under General George A. Stone of Iowa, Clarke's "young and beautiful daughter," having married General Stone.

He was one of the contractors of the old Pittsburgh, Cleveland and Ohio Railroad and also connected with the Michigan Central. It was a source of pride ot him that he furnished the rails for the first railroad built in Michigan which ran from Detroit to Ypsilanti. The rails were imported from England and brought up the rivers from New Orleans by Clarke.

Charles E. Clarke and his brother both died on the same day, Feb. 1, 1901, Frederick in DesMoines, Iowa and Charles in New Rochelle, N.Y. The Clarkes were reported to be distant cousins of both Generals Grant and Sherman. There was another brother, Julian Clarke, and their sister, Sarah Clarke Lippincott, who wrote under the name of Grace Greenwood.

Clark Street in Dowagiac was named for this family. One of the Clarke homes was said to be on East Division Street in that vicinity. There are a number of Clarke descendants still living in Dowagiac and vicinity.

46

Some Firsts

Patrick Hamilton made the first addition to the Village of Dowagiac in the spring of 1849, and laid out what was known as Hamilton's First Addition to the original plat as laid out by Beeson and Cheesebrough. He was followed in quick succession by Jay W. McOmber, Hamiilton's Second Addition and by Erastus Holmes Spalding.

Noel Hollister was the first resident lawyer.

The first wedding was that of Joel H. Smith and Sylvia Van Antwerp and who celebrated their Golden Wedding here.

The first birth was that of a son born to Mr. and Mrs. Hulemisky while the father was working for the railroad. He was given a village lot but the family did not remain here.

The first girl born was Fannie Wares, afterwards Mrs. C.J. Greenlead.

Arad Balch was the first postmaster and M.T. Garvey the first justice of the peace.

Justus Gage was the first village president, elected in 1858; and Freeman J. Atwell the first city mayor, elected in 1877.

H.B. Denman established the first bank here in 1856, called The First National Bank. The day book of that bank, at least for the first year or two is in existence here in Dowagiac.

The first lodge established here was the IOOF Lodge No. 57 on September 12, 1851.

47

Citizens of Dowagiac

Dowagiac, as well as Cass County, has for well over a century, been the home of many black residents, who have always been active and highly respected residents of this community.

While many have their own churches, others have become welcome members of other denominations in the community. These people were very early members of the old First Baptist Church here, before they decided upon their own church, the Second Baptist Church, which celebrated its 100th anniversary close to 20 years ago. Although there has been no First Baptist Church since 1918, the members have always retained the name, "Second Baptist Church." The church originally was located on the corner of West Division and Pennsylvania Ave. A new church was built on Paul St. when the former location was acquired by the post office.

The people of this race have served in their country's armed forces beginning with the Civil War and in all succeeding conflicts—have served on the city council and the county board and held other offices—they have long ago made a place for themselves as part and parcel of this community.

There have been many outstanding citizens among them and older residents will remember Thomas Jefferson Martin who came to Dowagiac in 1855 and became one of its most prominent and active citizens.

He was an excellent orator and when debating was a popular indoor sport here, he always headed one of the teams and could hold his own against anyone. His father was William Martin, a United

States Senator from Tennessee.

In his obituary published in The Daily News on July 25, 1912, it failed to mention that he established a school in southern Indiana for black children. This was one of his many accomplishments.

"Thomas Jefferson Martin, Dowagiac's veteran barber and old time resident, who died yesterday afternoon at his home on Green street, bore an intreresting and notable career.

"His mother, a Tennessee slave, his father a full blood white planter, he grew to manhood with an intimate knowledge of early slave conditions in the south and made his way to the north and freedom in an early day, and became a barber by occupation and an abolitionist in sentiment and thought.

"He was reared until he reached the age of 21 years at Florence, Alabama. His master was kind to him and in the year of 1832, he was set free at the age of 13 years. He was then bound out to learn the barber trade and completed this education at the age of 21.

"On reaching his majority he was compelled to leave the state of Alabama as there was a state law prohibiting free Negroes from living there.

"He went from Alabama to New Orleans, and later to Madison, Ind., and at the latter place was married. One child, C. Fabe Martin (Cyrus Fabius) was born to this union.

"For a great many years, from the time that he landed in New Orleans and until he went to Madison, Ind. to live, Mr. Martin worked on the steamboats which plied the Ohio and Mississippi Rivers. There he met many men of renown, shaving, while a barber on the river boats, many men of national prominence. It is said that while thus employed on the Mississippi River that Abraham Lincoln at one time occupied his barber chair. After quitting the river life he became connected with the underground railroad system which carried escaping slaves from the slave states, through the north to Canada and to freedom. He was finally detected while assisting runaway slaves and was compelled to get away from the border.

"He then came to Kalamazoo in the year 1854, and from Kalamazoo to Dowagiac, October 5, 1855. He has lived in Dowagiac ever since.

"While the date of his birth is given as June 22, 1820, making him 92 years old, but he is believed to be older than this, as his date of birth was somewhat shrouded in mystery.

"During all of the years of his residence here, Mr. Martin was a familiar figure, not only of local reputation but state wide. He was prominent in the African Masonic lodge, both state and national. In an early day he also took much interest in politics. A marked characteristic of his, was the old "stovepipe hat" of the Abraham Lincoln style which he wore for years. He also carried a cane.

"The funeral services will be held in the First Baptist Church at 2 p.m. tomorrow. Rev. Randall will officiate. Burial will take place in Riverside Cemetery."

His son, Cyrus Fabius Martin, known as "Fabe," was a gifted writer and poet. A play he had written came to the attention of a well known Broadway acress, who wrote to him and invited him to come to New York as she was interested in appearing in it. He did not go becaue he did not want her to know he was black. Had it been today it would have made no difference.

This was told to me by the late Atty. James H. Kinnane for whom I worked and who was a good friend of "Fabe." I have put away somewhere, the poem he wrote for me at the time of my marriage.

48

Renesten

Would Dowagiac be here today if William Renesten hadn't come along in 1830 to make use of the water power of the Dowagiac Creek at just the exact place he chose, a few rods from the east city limits of Dowagiac? Perhaps some other enterprising young man might have come along—but it was William Renesten who can rightfully be considered the founder of Dowagiac.

He had previously made a scouting trip to this community prior to 1830 from his home in Wayne County, Indiana. He was born in Mifflin County, Pennsylvanis in 1796. It was practically wilderness here except for the Potawatomi Indians who camped at intervals along the Creek to fish. The first white settlers had come a scant few years before in 1825.

Renesten went back to Indiana and brought his card machines in wagons and built a carding mill. It was an arduous trip as very few roads existed. People were flocking into Michigan from the east and Renesten could foresee there would be many coming here.

Three years later—in 1833—he built a grist mill at the same place, the irons for which were made at Cincinnati and brought by wagon, a distance of some 200 miles. The burrs were quarried and dressed near Elkhart. He had made preparations for this mill the year before by building a dam which created the present Dowagiac millpond. The original dam was south of the present location and below the hill on which Old Mill Farm house stands, and just south of M-62. The imprint, pointed out by the late Dr. Jesse Ritter, great-grandson of William Renesten, is still there.

A saw mill was established on the dam in 1834. Settlers wanted to be near the mills and soon a little settlement existed and became what is now Dowagiac. Old LaGrange Township records show that the present Dailey Road which ends at M-62, was ordered built "to Renesten's carding mill," as well as other roads which were then trails through the woods, including M-62. It is possible that William Renesten might have been influenced by the fact that the Grand River Indian Trail, an important trail, came through here, although he did not build on it, needing the water power.

By 1836, the Indian trail was made into a road, coming down over Henderson Hill into what is now Dowagic. M-51 South follows it most of the way to Niles. Stagecoaches were soon traveling over it regularly, bringing landseekers by the hundreds.

But William Renesten grew tired of the mills and sold them to Erastus Holmes Spalding. He had built his home "on the high bank" across the creek, now Old Mill Farm. His son-in-law, Lyman Barker Spalding and daughter, Mary Renesten Spalding lived with the Renestens, starting their married life there. He moved to his farm in LaGrange Township, where Candace Townsend Spalding Kemp lives and where he farmed for 40 years. He died in his late 80's at the home of his daughter, Melinda Ritter across the line in Berrien County.

William Renesten is buried in Riverside Cemetery, overlooking the community he helped to found—but not a single road, path, park or spot is named for him today.

But William Renesten was a legend in his own time, delightfully eccentric. He lived the way he pleased and others could do the same. He was well liked by his neighbors and by everyone who knew him.

Renesten collected clocks and he kept a clock in every room and all were kept running. He enjoyed the startled looks of visitors when every clock in the house began striking off the hour. A great-grandson, Dr. Harold Hain, had one of these old clocks.

He also collected old harnesses and various types of farm tools which filled one barn on his farm.

A couple of secrets died with William Renesten. One story is told of him, that once a boy in the neighborhood chopped a big gash in his foot. The boy's brother was sent flying by their mother to "Uncle Billy" Renesten's to find out what to do. He was sitting in front of his fireplace. He said nothing for a minute, but picked up a poker and began stirring it around in the ashes. Finally he looked up and said, "You can go home now, it has stopped bleeding." When the boy returned home, it had.

Another story has been handed down in the Wright family, pioneer settlers of La Grange. Stephen Wright, ancestor of the local family, complained one day that he was being overrun with rats, they were in the house and he couldn't seem to get rid of them.

William Renesten told him he could get rid of them but first he should write down on a piece of paper the name of someone he disliked. Stephen Wright was a Quaker and a kindly man with no enemies. He could think of no one but was finally pressed into writing down the name of a man living in the township.

William Renesten took the piece of paper. After awhile he came back with a letter he had written, went upstairs in the Wright home and placed it in the attic. The rats suddenly left and Stephen Wright was bothered no more.

One day, not too long after this incident, Wright met the man whose name he had written down on the piece of paper. The man remarked: "The strangest thing happened to me," and went on to say that an army of rats had suddenly invaded his house and barn. Stephen Wright asked him when it had happened. It was the day after William Renesten had written a letter to the rats.

He would only laugh when questioned about these things, his bright blue eyes twinkling with amusement. He would just shake his head and say, "Some day before I die I will tell you," but he never did.

49

Nicholas Bock

Nicholas Bock, one of Dowagiac's earliest residents, lived a most colorful existence during the more than 45 years he spent in this community. It might be due to the fact that he was born in Belgium and at the age of 15 was serving as a water boy in Napoleon's army at the Battle of Waterloo.

As a widower he came to America with his young son, Henry Bock, grandfather of Nick Bock of Dowagiac. He married twice more and among his children were Mary Bock Larzelere, mother of Harry and Arthur Larzelere, and Rose Bock Blackmond, mother of Fred and Ollie Blackmond.

In the beginning he was a farmer and was known to have been here as early as 1840 as his daughter, Mary Bock Larzelere was born on July 14, 1840 on a farm near Dowagiac.

He is best known as an inn keeper building Dowagiac's first hotel on West Division Street and Front in 1849. The American House was Silver Creek's voting place in the very early days. Here Dowagiac's first village election was held in 1858 when Justus Gage was elected village president.

Many other events took place here and dances were held on the second floor. Nicholas Bock was a popular landlord.

He was said to have sold the first liquor ever sold over a bar in Dowagiac. He soon became disgusted with this business because of the frequent drunken brawls and soon quit selling it.

Settlers coming to the community usually spent their first days at the American House. Other hotels sprung up, A.J. Wares building a hotel a little later. But the American House seems to have been the center of activity in very early days of the village.

The late J.R. Edwards many years ago told The Daily News of eating meals there in the 1860's. He remembered well the huge cast iron stove which was used to heat it. This stove was a mammoth affair, built of cast iron blocks, and using three-foot wood.

It was molded by Owen Deal, who in those days operated a foundry at Whitmanville, as Lake LaGrange was then called. When once hot this stove would retain its heat for 24 hours without another fire.

In the early days Indians coming to town, rather than try to go home to Silver Creek after dark, would roll up in their blankets and lie down on the floor beside this stove.

The hotel was Silver Creek Township's voting place in the early days before Dowagiac became incorporated as a village. Because the hotel was located but a short distance from the four corners where Silver Creek, LaGrange, Wayne and Pokagon Townships meet, it was said that occasionally a voter was apt to go into the hotel and vote although he lived in one of the other townships.

Nicholas Bock had a hand in many things, farming and ownership of the old Red Mill in Silver Creek which was recently razed. This mill was built in the mid-1850's on what is now M-152 and known in the early days as "String Street."

The old Bock home is the big brick house located at 104 Oak St. The first house there was burned and Bock replaced it with the brick structure. Here he lived from time to time, giving up the management of The American House. However he couldn't quite give up being landlord, and named this residence "The National House," and operated a hotel there for a time. This, it is said, happened more than once. He died here in 1885.

50

Justus Gage

Justus Gage is another pioneer to whom the Dowagiac community owes much, and for whom the school district named one of its elementary schools.

A native of New York state, he came to this community in 1837 with his wife, mother-in-law, two children, and his brother, Ebenezer Gage and his family. Justus Gage's recital of their arrival and the first year of their stay here, was contained in detail in the 1948 Centennial Edition published by The Daily News.

In his memoirs he mentioned Dowagiac as "the little settlement on the mill dam," which the party passed as they proceeded to their land in Wayne Township. Justus Gage's farm home, which burned many years ago, was on what is now the Rudy Road. "Wilderness Farm," the home of the Samuel Johnson family and the late George R. Fox, he built for his daughter, Maria and her husband, which they never occupied, because of the death of Maria's husband, Horace McKeyes.

Justus Gage was ordained as a Universalist minister in New York at the age of 21, and after he came here he was a circuit rider for the church all over this area. His health failing, he moved into Dowagiac in 1857, and sold insurance.

The following year—1858, he was elected Dowagiac's first village president, the year the village was incorporated. He helped organize the Union School District in Dowagiac. He was one of the school inspectors who met in Patrick Hamilton's home in April, 1840 and established the first tax-supported public school in what is now

159

Dowagiac.

He was postmaster of Wayne Township, school teacher, justice of the peace, and supervisor of both Wayne and Silver Creek Townships. He was one of the organizers of the Dowagiac Universalist Church, now St. Paul's Episcopal Church, and taught in its Sunday School until his final illness in 1875. He also was one of the founders of the Cass County Republican, a newspaper published in Dowagiac.

He was president of the first Cass County Fair, and was the main speaker at the State Agricultural Society in the 1850's.

However, one of his greatest achievements was to introduce the resolution which brought Michigan State University into being, and served on its executive board for eight years.

And all this was done while he and his wife were both confirmed invalids, but nothing seemed to prevent him from serving this community. He took a deep interest in its affairs until the day he died.

By his will, his daily journals and correspondence concerning the college was left to his eldest son, DeWitt Gage, who moved to Detroit with his family. This was not known until long after his death and those of his two daughters who left no descendants.

Michigan State University officials, through Dr. Madison Kuhn of the faculty, have searched for years in an attempt to find these journals but they apparently were destroyed. Grandchildren of his youngest son, Benjamin Franklin Gage, were contacted in recent years, but they knew nothing of them, and very little about their grandfather.

Three of Justus Gage's five children preceded him in death, Maria, Ruth Ann and William Harrison Gage. Mrs. Gage, formerly Matilda Tinkler, survived her husband by several years. All are buried in Riverside Cemetery.

51

Patrick Hamilton

There could be no history of Dowagiac, even as incomplete as this one that fails to mention Patrick Hamilton often called the "Father of Dowagiac." He was not exactly the first white resident here -- his brother, George preceded him by a few months. William Renesten had lived in the community for five years, prior to Patrick Hamilton's arrival in 1835. Hamilton built one of the first homes in Dowagiac, and which is now located on Cross Street, and remodeled by Mr. and Mrs. Irving Johnson into an attractive, modern home.

Patrick Hamilton was born in Berkshire County, Mass. in 1794, his parents both dying when he was small. When he was 15 he and his brother, George took up land in Pennsylvania. They came to Comstock, Michigan and in 1835 to this community where Patrick bought 200 acres of land in Silver Creek, which included a part of what is now Dowagiac. He platted many lots in the city in his Hamilton additions and soon almost all of his original farm was within the city limits.

He gave land for various purposes including the old city cemetery. He helped organize the city, assisting churches and schools. It was in his home in 1840 that Dowagiac's first school was organized. It was then a Silver Creek Township school, with three other townships participating. He lived briefly in a log house on Center Street and then built a frame house on West Telegraph opposite Center St. This home was moved to Cross Street and where the Johnsons now live. The Congregational Church was organized in this house in 1849, and he remained an active member all of his life.

He was a generous man and helped many a man get a start in life by loaning him money. He never foreclosed a mortgage but always gave a man plenty of time to repay him.

This is the man for whom the Patrick Hamilton School was named. He served many years as a school trustee and was also on the village council.

52

The Hamiltons

Although Patrick Hamilton has often been called "the father of Dowagiac," his brother, George Hamilton and his wife, Elizabeth Sheldon Hamilton, came first to what is now Dowagiac in 1835. With them came their two-year old son, Abel Hamilton.

According to a story told to The Daily News by Abel Hamilton around the year, 1904, he stated that his father's house was the only one in the vicinity, and dense woods covered what is now Dowagiac. He was born in Pennsylvania in 1833. The family settled on the south bank of the Dowagiac River on a farm now covered by the Bassett Addition to Dowagiac.

Patrick Hamilton came soon afterwards and settled on this side of the river. Others soon followed including Elias Simpson; Jacob, Adam and John Muffley who settled on what was later the Henry J. Bock farm. Also early settlers were Jacob Stoff and Ira D. Mosher.

"George Hamilton ground many a bushel of corn by cutting a hole in a block of wood and crushing the grain with a round stone. When the Spalding mill was built he carried on his back to the mill a bushel of corn, walking around by the present cemetery, for there were no bridges except the one used by the stage coaches, down the river, although there was a beaver dam where the old brewery used to stand and it was possible to ford the river there and get across the marsh land safely.

"There were several children in George Hamilton's family and they with the Jarvis children—Burton, Zadock and Norman—went to school in a log schoolhouse on the present Hiram Dillman farm, three miles south of here, and it stood so thickly surrounded by trees, that a wind could have blown 20 of them onto the building, had it been strong enough.

"Thode Witherell taught this school and the children sat on benches made of basswood logs, split and so high from the floor their feet would not touch it.

"The nearest trading point was Niles and their crops were drawn there by an ox team, where they were floated down the river to St. Joseph. The grain was threshed with these same cattle, on a space of ground cleared for the purpose, and the chaff was gotten out with quilts.

"Mr. Hamilton's recollection is that the two political parties were Tories and Whigs. His father went to vote in those days in the schoolhouse on the late John K. Emmons farm. (This would be the Peavine School.)

"There was a road which skirted the river on the south, and one which came down through Wayne and crossed the river below here. These two roads joined at the Muffley place and went on to Niles.

"Game was plenty, and the river was full of fish. The Indians came and went, always respectful and friendly, and they as well as all the settlers called the river the 'Do-wah-gi-ake,'' the g being hard as in guide.

After Patrick Hamilton came the location attracted others, and James McOmber settled on the present McOmber place; Eli Veach located at the Arbor Crossing; Elder Watson settled on the site of Charles Avery's farm, and a Mr. Defoe bought the land now occupied by the King Addition.

"To visit with any of these the families had to ford the river, and this they did often, for the McOmber place (corner of North Front and Prairie Ronde Streets) was for years a stopping place for the sttage coach, and dances, shooting matches, etc. were of common occurrence there.

"Lawsuits were seldom heard of in those days. Silas P. Howell was the first justice of the peace within his recollection. He settled on the present Peter Hannan farm in the early '40's, and James McOmber, always well dressed and wearing a plug hat, usually appeared on one side or the other, and pettifogged—and sometimes befogged for his client.

"Mr. Hamilton's father and mother, two brothers and a sister are buried on the farm they came to so long ago, in the corner of the field near the Dayton Cushing place. (This would be what is now the old Pokagon St. Cemetery. The land was later owned by the Burling family, and the cemetery is often called the Hamilton Cemetery.)

"Abel Hamilton worked for his uncle Patrick, and later spent a short time in Wisconsin. With this exception he has always lived here.

"He remembers when the town was named and remembers the men who came here to make its early history. He has two sons and three daughters and lives happily with one—Marion—his wife having gone before."

53

Noahdia Potter

When Noadiah Potter died in 1909 at the age of 95 in Dowagiac, he was one of Cass County's oldest residents. He was a gunsmith and guns made by Potter are collector's items today. The museum at Michigan State University has one.

Born in Cincinnati, Ohio, he first came to Cass County to Porter Township in the 1830's, and after the arrival of the Michigan Central to Dowagiac in 1848, came here. He first lived on High Street, then on South Front occupying the site at the corner of South Front and High Street of the former Powell Hotel. He later moved to a building on the site of the present Masonic Temple and from there to Commercial Street where the Community State Bank is located.

A gunsmith was a necessity in the early days, and he never lacked for work. His son, Frank was a blacksmith here, and was located on Pennsylvania Avenue in the block south of Commercial Street.

The latter's son, Ray "Pete" Potter followed in his father's footsteps.

54

Daniel McOmber

Much has been written about Daniel McOmber and other members of the McOmber family who were residents of the Dowagiac area before there was a Dowagiac. They established the McOmber tavern on the northwest corner of what is now North Front and Prairie Ronde Streets and were prominent in public affairs.

But very little has been written about Daniel McOmber's adventures in the west. This story, probably written by Julius Becraft, owner of The Dowagiac Republican, appeared July 11, 1895:

"Daniel M. McOmber, a white-haired old man, rugged and sound in constitution despite his years, was seen by the Republican at his home in the Northern part of the city and questioned regarding his personal recollection of Marcus Whitman, the famed pioneer. His heroic action in behalf of Oregon is so well known to students of history and whose figure is at present occupying a deal of attention in current thought.

" 'I emigrated to Oregon in company with Brookfield Gard, in October of the year 1845,' said the old man, 'and we settled near Oregon City.

" 'I first met Whitman in 1847 when I was building a threshing machine -- the first ever built west of the Rocky Mountains, by the way -- and he came out to examine the machine and offer suggestions concerning its construction. He was a well-built man, of fine physique, about five feet ten, and having a finely formed head. He was then superintendent of all the missions in Oregon and it was at this period that his most efficient work in civilizing the Indians was done.

" 'It was in Novmeber, 1848, one year after his memorable lonely ride to Washington that will make him famous in history that he was murdered by the Indians. He was then stationed with his family on the Walla Walla River, 20 miles south of Fort Walla Walla.

" 'The causes that led to the horrible massacre are as follows: There was much jealousy and dissension existing between the Indians of Catholic and Protestant missions and this was fanned by the agents of the Hudson Bay Company, an English company who were anxious to get Whitman out of the way.

" 'Whitman, besides being a minister and a skilled mechanic, was a physician and doctored the Indians when an epidemic broke out. The direct cause of their outbreak was this: Medicine was left for two Indians who were ill, by one of whom it was refused. The one who took the medicine died and the ignorant savages, believing Whitman had poisoned him, planned his massacre. Thjey waited until all the other inmates of the mission were absent, then rushed in and killed him.

" 'The excitement caused among the early settlers there by the news of his murder was intense. An army was at once formed to avenge his death, of which I had the honor to be a member. We were in active service fighting the Indians about nine months.'

"Mr. McOmber's reminiscences of his early experiences in the west are indeed very interesting. He was one of the party who first crossed the one road over the Cascade range of mountains when the road was first built. It was cut out by a private corporation. Many interesting ancecdotes he tells of wild life and thrilling experiences in that uncultivated wilderness. He was intimately associated with the early growth of the region and his testimony is of great interest."

55

H.B. Tuthill

The late Judge H.B. Tuthill in October, 1932, wrote up his memoirs as relating to his early days in Dowagiac and Keeler. The family came here in 1854. Tuthill Street in this city was named for Cyrus Tuthill. Judge Tuthill touched upon all aspects of life in the early days of Dowagiac that will be of interest to many. He wrote:

Many of the early settlers of Dowagiac and vicinity, and this statement is true of Southwestern Michigan as well, came from the East, from New York, and from New England. They brought and suffused a culture which survives.

Mrs. Tuthill's ancestors and also my ancestors came from the East—from New York, and from New England to New York. The stock was, and still is, good—we know.

Becoming acquainted, my parents married in 1852. The trek to Dowagiac was in 1854. There my father continued merchandising in partnership with William R. Sturgis, in the store building, being a frame one, on the west side of Front Street opposite Beeson Street. This building, with adjoining ones, was destroyed in the big fire of 1863. My parents, while in Dowagiac, lived in the ell of the house afterwards occupied by Thomas J. Martin. There my sister, Annie and I were born. Mrs. Tuthill was born on the old Wells farm in Wayne.

Across the road, as all highways were then denominated, from where our parents resided, lived the family of Joseph B. Clarke, (206 Green St.) who will be remembered as a prominent and successful lawyer. In those days Grace Greenwood, a sister of Mr.

Clarke, was budding into prominence. She came west quite frequently and was intimately acquainted with all of the old time people of the then hamlet. (Sarah Jane Clarke Lippincott).

In 1862 the firm of Tuthill and Sturgis closed its Dowagiac store. We moved to Hartford, then also a hamlet where my father carried on merchandising for a year. I remember our sojourn in Hartford; and especially the large number of Indians who came in from the reservations both north and south. In 1862 we moved on a farm in Keeler Township, in what was then known as the Roosevelt-Baker-Felt-Conklin neighborhood. There for three years we lived in a log house. In my childhood memory lingers a recollection of the spendid times those people indulged. The banquets, prepared and served by the ladies, were truly fine, and much enjoyed by all.

One afternoon I was in the front yard of our Keeler home. The wind was in the north, the weather was cold and raw. I observed a neighbor, William Conklin driving westwardly toward our house. He "hoyed up" near the rail fence and addressing me said, "Harry call your mother." Upon my mother's appearance Mr. Conklin exclaimed, "Mrs. Tuthill, Abraham Lincoln has been assassinated." I had never heard that term before, but one look into my mother's face and I read the definition. Northern bickerings were forgotten. For there were Copperheads in the north, as there were secessionists in the south. The world, appalled, stood still.

With the advent of the Michigan Central Railroad times picked up, and the little hamlet of Dowagiac increased importantly, for it was in the center of a large wheat area. After harvest and in the fall months on many days, 300 wagon loads of wheat would pass eastwardly on Beeson Street to the freight house bridge, thence up the incline and unload into a hopper which deposited the wheat in the bins below.

There were three crossing of the Dowagiac Creek marshes, the upper, middle and lower crossings. One due north on the town line road between Wayne and Silver Creek, one diagonally through Silver Creek, and one on the line between Silver Creek and Pokagon.

Each one was nearly one mile in length, that being the approximately width of the marsh. (Note: It must be remembered that in the early days the Dowagiac marsh was much larger and greatly reduced later by a drainage project.) The traveled portion was over a corduroy road. I have heard my father remark that "travelers riding a skittish horse were obliged to lead him over, as once off the corduroy the horse and rider would sink out of sight in the mire."

The fall of 1865 we moved to the old farm west of Dowagiac. The evening of the first day of our arrival was warm, the moon was full, a soft wind blowing from the south wafted to our ears a rumbling noise. Soon off across the prairie we discerned flickering lights through the trees, the dim front of a Michigan Central miniature engine came into view; the tender filled with wood followed, and then other flickering lights. And progressing slowly, as did all trains in those years, it finally groaned to a stop at the old station of the Michigan Central then on the east side of the tracks, which station house was afterwards moved to and became a part of Mark Judd's planing mill.

As the train came to a pause, the Silver Cornet band struck up a patriotic air, and on the hill to the westward, as the sound rose, we heard the tremendous shouts of men, and the sobbing laughter of women. I inquired of my mother what all of this meant, and she replied. "The boys are coming home from the war." But many there were who did not return.

Perhaps a few persons now in life will remember that a few rods of where Front Street turns westwardly and becomes Pokagon Street there was in the early days an Indian cornfield. As were all Indian cornfields, it was round and covered perhaps an acre of land, and was surrounded by mammoth oak trees, hazel brush and other woods.

I remember that when we moved on the old farm west of town there were remaining evidences of two Indian mounds, constructed by some prehistoric race of men who lived long before those, we now speak of as aborigines, inhabited this country; and again there were evidences on the old farm, when the white man came, of an Indian village inhabited by the Potawatomis, or perhaps by some prior inhabitants. In the 15-acre field northeast of the house I have picked up, while working, five and perhaps more Indian arrowheads in one day, and one especially now in my possession I will mention. It is about one inch long, of pure quartz. The work is marvelous, especially when we consider it must have been fashioned by hand.

On the first Monday of December, 1865, my sister, Annie and I entered the Dowagiac schools. I was placed in the C class of the first primary where I remained for three months. Afterwards for two whole years in the second primary I was taught to count by ones, twos, threes, fours, fives, sixes, sevens, eights, nines and tens up to a hundred. The teacher afterwards began on the multiplication table, and we spent a couple of years on that. All of which I had been taught in that little white school house on the Territorial Road a mile and a quarter north of our Keeler home.

While we were in the second primary a fight occurred between two boys, I shall describe the fight in the language of the time. One boy was the son of a prominent citizen and a large taxpayer, who lived in a big house. The other boy was an oprhan "bound" to a nearby farmer. They finally came together. And in less than two minutes rich man's son had been so thoroughly trounced that he wabbled, whereas Dan had not even turned a whisker. Teacher observed whole affair, its beginning, its progress and its conclusion. She uttered no word of condemnation of rich man's son. Her language as she berated Dan, I still feel was scandalous. That teacher has been dead for many years. I still dislike her. I never visit her grave.

Dan Palmer, I repeat, was a bound boy. He received his meals and was given a place in the attic to sleep. Scantily clad he was compelled to work in all kinds of weather. He was however, allowed a few months schooling in the winter. Dan was stricken with quick consumption as that terrible disease was then known. My mother was with him frequently as also was I.

His body lies buried in that little graveyard on Pokagon Street, 60 rods west of its intersection with Front Street. His pallbearers were the four young men who graduated in the spring—if my memory serves me, of 1870.

The last year of school, 1877-78, Professor Tower was the superintendent, Miss Ingersoll the preceptress, Miss Drury the assistant. They taught us thoroughly and well, not alone through what the books contained, but also by observations and lectures regarding our duties throughout life. We admired them then. We are grateful to them now.

The English literature class was heard in the laboratory. Miss Drury was our teacher. We did not often recite. It was assumed we came prepared to do so. Who of the remaining few will ever forget her rendition of Canto Fifty—The Combat—forget The Lost Huntsman, FitzJames; the Scottish Chieftain, Roderick Dhu; their meeting; the journey, the sword fight and its conclusion. We ourselves have visited Scotland, Benledi still towers; the Vennachar is now a narrow brook; one may cross Coilantogle ford with ease; the memories of that long ago recital still linger.

And one must not fail to mention the Lyceum nor indeed its patrons. Bankers, preachers, business men, nearby farmers, attended often; and too, sometimes kindly assisted in the debates. I mention two especially, Mr. Martin and Mr. Wheeler, the one a barber, the other a blacksmith. For truly each was an orator.

One evening Prof. Thompson "made a slip" that "Queen Victoria occupies about the same position in English life that the American flag occupies in American life," and the row was on. John C. Dyson, the man of mystery and of many unexplained experiences; Prof. Slater the boy orator; Dr. Marr, the Rev. A.S. Kedzie; Henry Straub, the profound thinger; Thomas J. Martin, James Wheeler, and perhaps some other lesser lights joined in the fray. Many vital issues were drawn into the debate; they fought the war all over again; they settled the Indian question; and the Land Grant problems; they trenched upon the Missouri Compromise. Oratory waxed and waxed again until midnight.

I studied law with Spafford Tryon whom I always greatly admired. He could enunciate and define legal principles in the fewest words of anyone I ever knew.

One October morning in the year 1878, John Tryon and I had arrived at the office. The door was soon opened, and in walked a young man, his face suffused with that smile so familiar to the then and after residents of Dowagiac. John Tryon's lips also parted and a smile spread over his face as he inquired, "Is this Coy?" (Coy Hendryx). That day began a friendship which continued for nearly 54 years.

Frank ReShore and I were examined in the old court house at Cassopolis on the evening of December 2, 1879. The Honorable

Andrew J. Smith presided as judge. The committee consisted of Harsen D. Smith, Marshall L. Howell, each of Cassopolis, Lester A. Tabor of Lawton.

The examination for admission consumed three hours, from 7 to 10 p.m. At the conclusion of the examination Mr. Tabor requrested permission of the court to ask one more question. That question was, "What is the first duty of a lawyer after admission" Having been reared on a farm and being rather unsophisticated I did not know. Frank, the old sleuth, however, answered promptly, "To buy an oyster supper for the crowd." We did.

I repeat, the examination for admission to the bar was on December 2, 1879. On December 15th of that year we took up our residence in Michigan City. This is our home and here we shall remain.

The year 1871 was very dry, scarcely any rain fell during the summer. Many people thought the drought, more severe than theretofore experienced, was caused by a denuding of the forests. In the month of October occurred the Great Chicago Fire. A few days thereafter Will and Charley Hannan visited the scene of the disaster, and, returning regaled many crowds with accounts of what they had seen. These Hannan boys deserve more than mere mention. They peddled handbills; carried water for the elephants, created an enlarged desire for peanuts; made delicious candies which they sold. Saturday afternoons were big days for them, as all farmers have a sweet tooth. And they saved their earnings too. Years after both had become men, Charley informed me that when they reached the age of 21 years, each had accumulated five thousand dollars. The elder, Will, became a most successful dealer in Detroit real estate and bonds. The younger, Charles, became a banker in Council Bluffs, Iowa.

During the last year of attendance at school, John Burns (Byrnes) of Pokagon and I carried our lunch "in the pocket." We were much together. John Burns was dearly beloved by all. His observations were always pat and to the point. He was in Lyceum debates, coveted as a proponent and friend, by all others feared as an antagonist. His sudden death in 1880 cast a pall over all.

In the southwest corner of old Wayne in the early days lived

Justus Gage. We came to know him by reason of his frequent visits to the primary department. He used to talk to us. He did not offer advice—he reached and influenced us by suggestion. When present, which was often at chapel exercises, his reading of the Scripture lesson was impressive. His prayers came from the heart. He was, indeed, One Grand Man.

I cannot within the space allowable make mention of the many good men and true women who lived in Dowagiac during the years of my childhood and youth. I must not, however, forbear to mention Mr. Vincent, the school janitor. In those days I carried my dinner, and Mr. Vincent and I indulged in many long talks, or rather, he talked, I listened and profited much indeed.

And then that other old timer, Billy Smith, as we knew him. The family lived in a house on Commerical Street, below the Methodist church. Billy used to drive team for parties to "Poke," "Whit," "Cass" and many other points. He worked for the Hannan boys too, and on farms. He was always doing something. Afterwards the family removed to Grand Rapids. There he continued to work at anything that came along. He became perhaps the most successful and prominent of the old, or any modern crowd. He was general counsel for several Michigan railroad companies. He was a member of Congress many times. He was United States Senator for Michigan. He was the choice of several states for president of the United States. (William Alden Smith).

' Perhaps it is well known that the area of old Dowagiac, within the confines of Silver Creek, was laid out by Patrick Hamilton. Originally it was a part, or the whole, of his farm. I knew Mr. Hamilton as a child might know a prominent and influential citizen, by sight. He was rather tall, somewhat spare, very dark, always neatly dressed and wore a full beard. I do not remember that either hair or beard were tinged with gray. He never rode when it was possible to walk, and continued to be vigorous until near the close of life. He was a man of sterling intergrity, absolutely square in his dealings and trusted by all. Indulgent with his debtors, kind to the poor. Times were hard after the war, money scarce and hard to acquire. His humanity may be illustrated perhaps by the recital of a conversation I heard between two men years and years ago. "While Patrick

Hamilton lives there will be no foreclosure. He will give me time, and I can save my farm."

I must pause for a moment to speak of another old and dear friend, Henry Bock. Born a peasant in Belgium, he came to America with his father when young. My mother informed me that upon arrival she and my father boarded for a while at Bock's Tavern (American House built by Henry Bock's father, Nicholas Bock), and that Mr. Bock waited on them at table. Afterwards he joined a caravan of gold seekers to California, going by way of the Isthmus. We moved to a farm west of town and Mr. Bock and I became acquainted. I was with him often. I worked for him many times in harvest. Indeed, we were binding wheat in his field when a neighbor informed us of the Custer Massacre. Mr. Bock always paid an honest wage for honest work. His portrait has occupied an honored place in my office for many years.

And I must not fail to speak of that dear friend, Mr. B.W. Schermerhorn, who was a justice of the peace for many years with offices in the old Jewell block on Commercial Street. While as a law student, it fell to my lot to try several small cases in court over which he presided. On several osccasions after both client and I had lost—client the amount of his alleged claim, and I what I had hoped for and did not receive, Mr. Schermerhorn would go over the latter and inform where where I had fallen down.

I might talk on and on of the old crowd—one more. While we lived in Keeler at threshing time, Frank McAlpine, a boy in his teens, "drove the horsepwer," and afterwards when older, fed the threshing machine and thereby suffered the loss of a hand and the forearm. He thereupon entered Dowagiac High School and graduated with honor. He taught for several years; became a clergyman; and afterwards departed this life universally loved and honored.

I cannot close this without touching for a moment on a subject which is very close and intimate. In the early years of the Second Primary I looked over the school and observed a little girl. We passed through the grades, through both intermediates into and through the high school—always in the same class. We attended the same church, the same Sunday School—we rarely spoke one to the other—no, not then. I came to Michigan City. She followed soon afterward. We still abide one with the other.

Before and at the time of her birth, and for several years afterwards, Mrs. Tuthill's parents, Mr. and Mrs. Henry B. Wells lived on the old farm in Wayne. In his young manhood Mr. Wells for several years was in control of the fuel supply for the Michigan Central Railroad. This was when the road extended no further west than Michigan City. Afterwards he furnished the piling used by that company, and the Illinois Central, in building the causeway from Sixteenth Street to South Water Street in Chicago. In those days the lake extended eastwardly as far as what is now the east line of Michigan Avenue, and the old railroad bed was 20 rods west of the shore line.

Subsequently as Superintendent of Construction for the State of Michigan, he aided in building the locks, then the largest in the world at the Soo. He also served as supervisor of Wayne Township and chairman of the board; member of the state legislature; merchant, and postmaster of Dowagiac when I came to know him.

56

King Gillette

There is hardly a mercantile establishment in the United States or most of the world for that matter, where the name "Gillette" doesn't appear, whether it is on a package of razor blades, a safety razor and many other men's toilet articles.

The is due to King C. Gillette, the inventor of the safety razor, who lived in Dowagiac community 100 years ago or more. He was even well known then for he was Dowagiac's champion roller skater.

As he once wrote to James Harley with whom he maintained a lifelong friendship, the Gillettes were always inventing something, his father, his brother, George and himself, and that the patent office had many Gillette inventions on its records.

An early invention of his might have been the forerunner of the safety razor, according to the late Roy Elliott of Dowagiac, a well known race driver and horse trainer in his day. He said that after King Gillette left Dowagiac he invented a pair of horse clippers, which Elliott said were by far the best on the market. He used them for many years in his business. He said that King Gillette traveled on the road selling his clippers and would stop in Dowagiac to visit his friends. Elliott also said that he used to go to the local skating rinks to watch King Gillette perform.

King Gillette was born January 5, 1855 in Fond du Lac, Wisconsin, the son of George and Fanny Camp Gillette. The family came to Dowagiac from Chicago, just when is not known, except that King Gillette was a boy. He said that his father lost everything in the Chicago fire of 1871.

The Gillettes lived about a mile outside the city on what was known as the Moore farm and now the Sedlar farm. The house there today is the same one in which the Gillette family lived.

The family must have been living here on and off before the Chicago fire for Fanny Gillette, author of the famous "White House Cook Book," was involved in several real estate transactions here, including the William C. Moore farm, a Dowagiac business block and another large farm which she sold for $18,000 in 1872. Although King Gillette said he had been on his own since he was 17 years old, the family wasn't exactly poor.

The Gillettes always maintained a close connection with Dowagiac, King Gillette with James Harley, and his mother, Fanny Gillette with the H.F. Colby family. She would occasionally visit the Colbys, and their daughter, Eleanor would go to Redlands, California to visit Fanny and her daughter, Fanny. The latter was a well known actress in her day. She first went on the road with John McCullough, and afterwards was a leading lady with Robert Mantell, Frederick Warde, and Lewis James, all famous Broadway actors.

Sometime before World War I or perhaps a short time afterwards, King Gillette paid one more visit to his boyhood home, and with his friends, Jim and Tom Harley attended a performance at the beautiful little Beckwith Memorial theater which he greatly admired.

In 1918 King Gillette wrote the history of the origin of the Gillette safety razor. "It was in 1895 in my 40th year, that I first thought of the razor, and to appreciate the causes that led to its conception, it is necessary that I should go back a little and become somewhat personal in regard to myself and my affairs.

"Until the fall of 1904, I was a traveling man and sold goods throughout the United States and England, but traveling was not my only vocation for I took out many inventions, some of which had merit and made money for others, but seldom for myself, for I took out many inventions, some of which had merit and made money for others, but seldom for myself, for I was unfortunately situated not having much time and little money with which to promote my inventions or place them on the market. My impulse to think and invent was a natural one, as it was with my father and brothers—as will be found in looking over the records of the Patent Office where we have a great many inventions to our credit."

King Gillette told how he was influenced by his employer in Baltimore who invented the Crown Cork—the tin cap with a cork lining for bottles. He urged King Gillette to invent something when once used is thrown away and the customer comes back for more. Years afterwards when Gillette showed him the model of the razor he was ill and unable to help King Gillette but told him, "whatever you do, don't let it get away from you."

King Gillette told how the idea for the safety razor was born. "I was living in Brookline (Mass.) at No. 2 Marion Terrace at that time (in the summer of 1895). On one particular morning when I started to shave, I found my razor dull, and it was not only dull but it was beyond the point of successful stropping and it needed honing, for which it must be taken to a barber or to a cutler.

"As I stood there with the razor in my hand, my eyes resting on it as lightly as a bird settling down on its nest—the Gillette razor was born. I saw it all in a moment, and in that same moment many unvoiced questions were asked and answered more with the rapidity of a dream than by the slow process of reasoning.

"A razor is only a sharp edge and all back of that edge is but a support for that edge. Why do they spend so much material and time in fashioning a backing which has nothing to do with shaving? Why do they forge a great piece of steel and spend so much labor on hollow grinding it, when they could get the same result by putting on edge on a piece of steel that was only thick enough to hold an edge?

"At that time and in that moment it seemed as though I could see the way the blade could be held in a holder; then came the idea of sharpening the two opposite edges on the thin piece of steel that was uniform in thickness throughout, thus doubling its service; and following the sequence came the clamping plates for the blade with a handle equally disposed between the two edges of the blade.

"All of this came more in pictures than in thought as though the razor were already a finished thing and held before my eyes. I stood there before that mirror in a trance of joy at what I saw. Fool that I was, I knew little about razors and practically nothing about steel . . . and could not foresee the trials and tribulations I was to pass through before the razor was a success. But I believed in it, joyed in it. I wrote to my wife who was visiting in Ohio, 'I have got it; our fortune is made,' and I described the razor and made sketches so she would understand. I would give much if that letter was in existence today, for it was written on the inspiration of the moment and described the razor very much as you see it today, for it has never changed in form or principle involved—in refinements only."

King Gillette then described his trials and tribulations and endless sketches made and still in the company's files. His main trouble was in getting the right type of steel and in getting capital. For nearly six years "I tried every cutler and machine shop in Boston and some in New York and Newark in an effort to find someone who knew something about hardening and tempering thin steel so it would keep its flatness and not be warped by strains. Even the Massachusetts Institute of Technology experimented and failed absolutely in securing satisfactory results."

Everyone he consulted advised him to drop it. "But I didn't know enough to quit. If I had been technically trained, I would have quit or probably would never have begun." Gillette said he was a dreamer "and that is the reason, and the only reason why there is a Gillette razor today."

In December, 1901 King C. Gillette and several associates re ; .d a room over a fish store at 424 Atlantic Avenue in Boston. The Gillette Company history says "they had formed a new company and needed the space as a factory to make a shaving device invented by Gillette, a Bookline, Massachusetts salesman."

Two years later, in 1903 he put his razor on the market, but sold only 51 razors and 168 blades. It suddenly caught on and in 1905 sales boomed and the company moved to larger quarters. A building was found on First Street (now Gillette Park) near Dorchester Avenue in South Boston and where the Gillette Safety Razor Company still remains today.

By 1917 razor sales had gone over one million a year and the blade sales at 120,000,000. At the outset of World War I the output of the factor went almost exclusively to men in the armed forces. Many had never heard of a safety razor before when they were issued a Gillette. During World War II again almost the entire output went to the men in the service.

Many additions and changes have been made since King Gillette's death in 1932. He had retired from the company some years before, and moved to California where his mother and sisters were living. His picture is probably one of the best known trademarks in the world, for in 1962 it had appeared on over 100 billion packages.

The Dowagiac Daily News on Sept. 28, 1911, published excerpts from a letter written to James Harley by King C. Gillette. James Harley's father, James Harley Sr., was a pioneer merchant in Dowagiac, coming here from New York City where Jim and Tom Harley, his sons were born.

"Your most welcome letter was received this morning and I want to say that it was strange that it should come at this time—because I have been thinking a lot about you lately—and about Dowagiac, and those never to be forgotten days when as you say we were boys together.

'I have talked about you and those good times, to my wife and boy and have been saying over and over again, 'I am going out t Dowagiac, to see Jim and talk over old times, and go over some of the old ground and see the old farm. But I suppose things have changed so that the old landmarks are gone.

"Mother, Lina and Fanny are living at the Park Avenue Hotel, corner 32nd and Park Avenue, New York. My mother is now 83 years old and doesn't look sixty. She is in good health and should live many years longer. George is married and has no children. (His brother). His wife is in Europe at present and he is stopping with his mother and sisters at the Park Avenue Hotel.

"Mott (another brother) is married, has two beautiful boys, 12 and 14 years. He lives at Garden City, Long Island.

"I have one boy who will be 20 years old in November. He will enter Yale College next year. At present he is fitting out for a trip in the wilderness of Maine with five other fellows.

"I am nailed fast to my business and have had very little vacation in years. I am president of my company, and we employ about 2,500 people in our factories. About 1,500 here in Boston, 500 in England, 300 in Montreal, Canada, and 200 in France.

"Our goods are sold in every city and town in every civilized country in the world. It is a wonderful success, but sometimes I regret the sacrifice of pleasure that follows in the wake of building up a large business. I would give the world to be a boy again, to have the power to enjoy like a boy. One loses that when they give up their life wholly to business and making money. Your father was a boy to the last.

"You are free Jim, why not jump on the train and come out here? Our family is small, only my wife, her old mother, my boys and myself. I want you to see this factory and its wonderful machinery. I want to take you out in the car and let you see what a beautiful city and suburbs we have. I want you to see my home, and above all I want to talk over old times. We will run over to New York and see mother, Lina, Fanny, Mott and George and have a great reunion.

"Write and say you will be here and I will arrange to come to Dowagiac soom. What's become of Charlie Hubbard, Ollie Hungerford, Fabe Martin and what is Tom doing? Write again and let me know all about everybody." (They did exchange visits and it was some time after this letter that King Gillette visited Dowagiac.)

Jim Harley commented how much he enjoyed visiting the Gillette home on Middle Crossing Road and what a wonderful mother King Gillette had.

In 1919 King Gillette was living in California and was backing a "new institution for the cure of neoplastic diseases," in Los Angeles and for which he purchased $150,000 of radium at the start. He died in California in 1932.

57

Flavia Defendorf

Some of the most interesting reminiescences about Dowagiac were provided by the late Flavia Huntington Defendorf, when she was 90 years old. An unusually keen and intelligent women, an avid reader, and physically active, she walked down to The Daily News to relate her memories of early Dowagiac to this reporter. She died five years later at the age of 95.

She was just five years old in October, 1852, when she and her parents, Mr. and Mrs. Asa Huntington and baby sister, Fanny stepped off a Michigan Central train in Dowagiac where she was to spend the remaining 90 years of her life. There were around 300 persons living in the village then. Her father was the first druggist here and they lived in rooms over the drug store located on the site of the present Masonic Temple.

Dowagiac's first fire of 1853 never seemed to make local histories but she remembered it very well. A man named Taylor had a print shop in a building about where the Beery Pharmacy is today. In those days many of the stores and churches were heated by long box stoves and which in time developed cracks in their sides. It was a cold February night and Taylor went to the depot to meet his wife who was coming to Dowagiac to join him. While he was gone sparks from the stove ignited a pile of kindling. It was the middle of the night and the whole building was ablaze before anyone saw it. Mrs. Defendorf remembered being roused from her sleep to flee the fire as their building was also burned.

Housing was a serious problem as every train was bringing new residents to Dowagiac. They went to the old Exchange Hotel run by Jim Lee on the site of the present Firestone store.

Others living in the block who also fled in the night included Ira Starkweather, Louis Atwood, Mrs. Stoll and her daughters, Mary and Sabrina, John Barney and his family, and Mrs. Clarissa Barney.

Asa Huntington then bought from Mrs. Fannie Wares, a little four-room house where Holy Maternity Catholic Church is now located, and here Flavia Huntington lived until her marriage to Harmon Defendorf.

Dowagiac was but a little country village and the villagers kept their own cows. In the day time they sent them to Pine Lake which Mrs. Defendorf said was considerably larger in those days. At night the cattle would come home to a little clearing on Jay Street and here they pawed and roared all night.

As families began to take more pride in their surroundings, picket fences were built around the dooryards and each night the family's personal cow found her way to her own home and slept out in the street in front of her owner's gate. Cows wore bells and as mosquitoes were thick, up and down the street all night long there was a constant tinkling of bells. Boys—being no different then than now—were not averse to appropriating the bells.

When the Huntingtons came to Dowagiac there was but one church building, the first Baptist Church built in 1852, although other churches held services. She used to go to choir practice with her father. There were no street lights and her father challenged her to a foot race down Spruce Street towards home. In the darkness she stumbled over a cow and started a rip-roaring stampede all over that part of the village.

Church going was the principal form of entertainment and everybody' went if they wanted to be considered respectable members of society. The Baptists used the Dowagiac Creek on South Front Street for baptizing. Mrs. Defendorf recalled five young girls going to be baptized. Sadie Cullom backed down and never entered church again.

The one-room school house on the site of the former First Methodist Church was used by the Congregationalists and Methodists, and she and her sister, Fanny were baptized there,

Flavia wearing a new white dress and black silk jacket. Fanny cried and embarassed her sister greatly.

The Universalist Church, now St. Paul's Episcopal Church, was built in 1859, the same year the first Methodist Church was built here. It was dedicated in January, 1860 and the whole town was thrilled over the arrival of the pipe organ from Boston. B.F. Root, a noted musician in Chicago, came to play it at the dedication. In the early days it was pumped by little boys who earned their spending money that way. One was Joseph Straub, a grandson of one of the first Universalist ministers.

The choir always sang in the gallery at the rear of the church. The first organist was Maria Heazlit Rix and another was Minnie Wheeler. Choirs from the other churches would come on Sunday evenings to join the Universalist choir, an event looked forward to all week.

When Abraham Lincoln was assassinated the church was draped in black. Choir members came dressed in black for the memorial service. Mrs. Defendorf remembered that when the school burned in 1859, the infants' class taught by Lottie Hills met in this church.

The Congregatinal Church, which joined with the First Baptist Church in 1918 and became the Federated Church, was built in 1855. This building burned in 1947. It looked considerably different in the early days. One woman was heard to remark that the steeple resembled a crocodile's tail. When the church was first built two long stoves were placed in the hall entrances on each side of the back of the church. Long stove-pipes extended from these two stoves in back up to the front. In the winter drippings constantly fell and basins had to be placed at intervals on the floor to catch the sooty deposits as they rained down.

Mrs. Defendorf laughed heartily over one incident she recalled, and which churchgoers then didn't think so unusual. When the church foundation was built, a hole was left in the rear of the church. In those days pigs as well as cattle roamed the streets and the pigs picked this vacant place for their home. All during the services their loud squeals accompanied the choir and all but drowned out the minister's sermon. And those sitting in the front pews had to vigorously scratch fleas.

The topography of Dowagiac has changed considerably since

those early days. The hills were much steeper and have gradually been graded down. Mrs. Defendorf was much amused by complaints of residents in the vicinity of Orchard, West Division and Pennsylvania where lakes formed after each rain. In the early days the hill on West Division was much steeper and the water would rise to the top of the hill beside what is now Beery's Pharmacy. A rowboat was kept at this corner and residents were rowed back and forth as a matter of course. Years later many residents wished they had that rowboat.

While attending school Mrs. Defendorf said that a girl named Ada Clarke brought choloroform to school one day and passed it around on the girl's side, telling them it was perfume. Several girls were overcome but Flavia Huntington was a druggist's daughter and knew what it was. She had to take Sarah Hawks home.

Ada Clarke was the daughter of Attorney Joseph Clarke, one of the village's first lawyers, and became well known as Ada Murray, the actress. The Clarkes at the time of this incident lived at 206 Green Street. Several of this family became known in the theatrical world.

Mrs. Defendorf said the first burial ground was among the grubs where Central Junior High School stands. She was about seven or eight years old when they moved ten bodies to the old City cemetery located near the present Heddon factory.

In those days coffins were never opened but covered with glass. She was at the old cemetery while they were moving bodies and walked up to one casket that had been placed on sawhorses and which contained the body of Thomas Bowling. Just then the glass caved in and she was enveloped in a cloud of yellow dust—all that remained of Thomas Bowling. Mrs. Defendorf was always of the opinion that all the bodies weren't found and that the bones of some of Dowagiac's first dead still lie beneath the earth of the school grounds.

Some of the early events she remembered was that because of its central location the village fire bell was placed on top of the Methodist Church and always rung for fires or other important occasions.

The town "pest house" was located in "Hopkinsville" that part of the city located in the vicinity of McKinley School, and where the 19th Michigan Infantry had trained. It was also where Mrs. Defendorf and her friends went for picnics and Maypole dances.

In the early days North Front Street was familiarly known as "Snake" Street due to its large population of blue racers and there was many a runaway due to horses being frightened by a snake.

Pickett's Hill was at the head of Chestnut Street and somewhere along its length was a tannery. High Street was the home of Harder's brewery. There was a bridge over the freight house where teams were driven over to unload their wheat, and which children used for snowslides in winter. Courtland Street was another favorite sliding palce.

The ague was a common ailment as the village was surrounded by swamps which came almost to the dooryards. Typhoid fever was also common. Mrs. Defendorf could remember that doctors were Bradon, Hale, Morris, Prindle, Beals, Roedell, Fosdick, Mulvane, Clarke and Seely, all practicing here and all kept busy.

Singing school was conducted in the depot in the winter and music meant a great deal to early residents.

She remembered the trains which had big cowcatchers in front and huge funnel-shaped smokestacks, and when the railroad only went as far as Michigan City.

There were four livery stables, Stebbins and Dennison on the corner of Commerical and Michigan Avenue; Jeff Gardner's stables were on the site of Harding's on Park Place; and Charles Hubbard's father had a livery stable on Pennsylvania Avenue where the Amersdorfer Wiltse Insurance Agency is now located; and William Larzelere a little later on North Front St. near the corner of West Division.

Mrs. Defendorf's memories of the dread Dowagiac swamp were very vivid and she remembered its evil reputation as a habitat for robbers and horse thieves.

58

Florence Cushman Milner

The following is the autobiography of Florence Cushman Milner as it relates to her eight years in Dowagiac, 1866-1874. The house where they lived is still there at 413 W. High Street. Dowagiac was settled by many New England families and this story tells of the Cushman family, typical of that day. Not only did Florence Cushman teach in Dowagiac at the age of 16, she was also the first librarian for the Ladies Library Association. She left here for Niles in 1874 and taught in various placed in Michigan for 44 years, retiring in 1916. Her last post was in the Harvard University library. Her autobiography was furnished by Mary-Maude Oliver of Champaign, Ill., a niece, and daughter of one of the twins mentioned hereafter.

by Florence Cushman Milner

When I was ten years old, in the year 1866, my father, who was a cabinet maker, employed by the Abbott-Downing Carriage Company in Concord, New Hampshire, was offered an opportunity to work at his trade in what, to a New Englander at that time, was "way out west." Accepting the offer, he moved his family to Dowagiac, Michigan.

Our new home was a tiny cottage, set well back from the street in a grove of oak trees which were tall enough to make our front yard a green canopied marquee. A porch ran along the front of the house, from this, a central door opened abruptly into a tiny parlor. To the left was a small room intended for a parlor bedroom. Back of the parlor was the dining room, with my parents' room opening out of it. Back of all was the kitchen, and, New England fashion, a woodshed attached. From the parlor the steepest of stairs climbed to the chambers under the sloping roof. My 3-year old twin sisters occupied one of the tiny rooms and the other was my castle.

The little room opening from the parlor played a small part in early training. Instead of using it as a guest room, my mother rather ambitiously called it "The Library," although the supply of books was limited to the corner whatnot and a small table. My own set of Lucy books, by the author of the famed Rollo series, which I had purchased with pennies hoarded over a long period of time, was on one of the shorter shelves, the purple and gold of their bindings untarnished.

Of the other volumes I have a fairly fixed picture although I did not read them all. There was a life of Louis Kossuth with a flag of gilt on the back, "The Planter's Victim," a Civil War story bound in red, "Life of Empress Josephine," and an illustrated "Life of Christ" by Farrar.

Best of all was my mother's autograph album, a square book bound in red leather. It contained sentimental steel engravings and much poetry, some quoted and some original, written in the precise, slanting penmanship of her young days. On the table was a large Bible, resplendent with gilt tooling and clasp. My father bought it at an auction and brought it home one day, rather apologetically, because my mother never quite approved of his weakness for auction sales. But I am sure it was a good one, for it has survived, clasp and all, even to this day, with births, marriages and deaths dutifully recorded.

Calling this a library gave to books a respected place in our home and a forward looking attitude toward reading, an example of my mother's constant struggle toward her ideals. No doubt she had visions of a book-lined room which was never to be hers, but as with everything else, she stood on tip-toe, and reached as high as she could.

Later, through the strictest economy, a piano was acquired. It crowded itself into this little room, which was thereafter called the "Music Room." The what-not and the Bible went into the parlor. My mother loved music. She had a very fine voice herself, and had high musical ambitions for me. She sacrificed greatly to give me lessons, but I proved a disappointment. Silence often proclaimed that practice was not going according to schedule and my mother, upon investigation, usually found me curled up with a book, sometimes under the piano where I had once or twice eluded her eye. Although I got as far as playing "The Storm" and "A Maiden's Prayer," my interest clearly did not lie in that direction so I was set free and the opportunity was passed along to the twins who at a very early age were practicing eagerly and later played in many two-piano concerts throughout the area.

In this little house my mother met her first real responsibility for the total care of the family and of the house. My grandmother had assumed much of the work in the east, so my mother and I learned together. I cannot think of any phase of housework we did not master, though tears of discouragement (and I suspect dislike) were often in her eyes as mistakes were made. There were none of the helpful appliances considered indispensible today -- not even an ice box. An occasional chunk of ice was purchased and wrapped in a piece of carpet and put in the cellar in a tub.

We learned to cook on an old black stove and a good arm to take the place of an electric mixer, to sweep with wet pieces of paper scattered to keep down the dust, and to clean without miracle helpers, to churn with a dasher but rewarded with such buttermilk as cannot be found through modern methods, and to make soft soap in an iron kettle over a fire in the back yard, with lye and grease conserved carefully. This was a tedious process and somewhat dangerous as I discovered one day when my dress caught fire from a spattering of the grease. Dishwashing was made endurable for me through learning poetry from a copy pinned over the kitchen sink.

Much of the family life during the long summer days was lived on the porch and under the trees. All the work that could be carried outdoors was done there and the supper table, wheneve weather permitted, was spread under the sheltering oaks. Back of the house was an acre of ground. This was my father's garden which he cultivated with me close at his heels. I learned to plant all common vegetables. I learned the characteristic way each sprouted, grew and came into full fruition. We fought potato bugs constantly and valiantly. I learned so much from this quiet man, my father, without knowing that I was doing anything but spending many happy hours with him. The harvest of this companionship was a keen interest in all the intricate details of inanimate life and a sensitiveness to their beauty although my father never prated of beauty.

Limited means made it necessary for my mother to do most of her own sewing in addition to the general housework and I realized much later how very difficult it was for her to adjust to this routine. A new dress was achieved through the strictest economy and much labor, for dresses in those days were feats of engineering, the flower-sprigged dainty organdy that she was working on one day was nearly finished. It was made over a heavy waist lining to assure the firm close fit then in fashion. The seams were boned and carefully overcast, all by hand, of course.

At the last, the lining was to be cut low, leaving only the sheer material over the shoulders. In doing this, the scissors not only bit through the lining but through the organdy also. The waist, with its many bonings and feather stitching of seams and overcasting was a wreck. For an instant my mother looked aghast, but she did not give away to any outward lament. I can see her now, almost at the instant, reached for new material and began cutting out a new waist. I was but a child at the time, but throughout my long life, when faced with disappointment, that picture comes to mind to give me courage.

Another example of my mother's spirit when faced with a distasteful task comes to mind. For a time, we kept a cow. My mother had had no experience with animals and hated everything that had to do with the care of them. When my father, who did the milking, was taken ill, there was no one to perform this necessary task, so, as always, my mother rose to the occasion. The cow was tied to the fence and I was stationed at her head to see that nothing happened to the knot. It was a hot summer night and flies were a torment. My twin sisters, little as they were, were put on the other side of the fence to take turns holding the cow's tail through the bars to keep her from switching it in my mother's face.

My mother took the stool and attacked the milking. To some it may be a comical picture, and I will admit that, at this distance, my sisters and I are able to laugh about it, but we did no laughing then. That badly tethered cow, the pinioned tail, three children all deathly afraid of the cow, and my mother equally so, but with her head resting on the cow's flank while tears streamed down her cheeks as she tried to do her best as a supremely disagreeable task, did represent tragedy then. In spite of tears and terror, the job was done somehow, and none of us, including the cow, was the worse for the experience.

After we had been in Michigan for a few years, my grandmother finally decided to take the risk of venturing into this far western country to pay us a visit. My parents tried to persuade her to live with us, but nothing could induce her to live "the primitive life on the frontier." She was certain Indians still threatened and that the requirements of a respectable life were not yet possible.

To her, west was west, and the fact that our little town was on the direct line of the Michigan Central Railroad from Detroit to Chicago, had no power to change her mental picture. This idea must have persisted in spite of my mother's reassuring letters because when she finally did arrive, she brought a kerosene lamp, supposing that we were using candles. When she saw our tiny but comfortable house, she looked about in surprise and remarked, "Why Eliza you do look real cozy."

During the long perspective of years, this grandmother stands out in strong relief. As a child, I had no affection for her. She possessed none of the usual grandmotherly traits, was sharply critical of my actions and often was an obstructionist that stood between me and some childish heart's desire. She was born "way down in the state o' Maine in a small town near the Aroostic line. She always called herself a New Englander but she also took great pride in the strain of French blood that gave sparkle and vivacity to every word and action. This was probably why she never became a sit-by-the fire type of grandmother but went alertly and efficiently about her household tasks to the very last day of her 85 years.

She belonged to an age when caps were in vogue but she wore hers with a difference. They were of black lace with nodding flowers or bows of bright silk ribbon. I never remember seeing her with the then black silk apron for afternoon. No apron for her except for housework. She probably wore spectacles but her brillient eyes sparkled through them in a way to eclipse any glasses. She was also very fond of a dress that she could wear "to mill or meetin'."

On moral questions she knew no compromise, and if I was not a pattern of rectitude it was no fault of hers. She never failed of the sharp goad of some terse saying to drive me in the way I should go. After I left home and was beyond her shafts, my admiration and even affection for my grandmother grew throughout the years. It is with warm pleasure that I remember her intellect and keen wit as she retained that ability to aim her arrow of proverbs at the center of sham whenever she thought she saw it, to the last day of her life.

In winter after the dishes were cleared away, the dining room was the family rallying place. The lamp was placed in the middle of the table and beckoned to many quiet evenings. As my sisters grew older, they were allowed to stay up for a longer and longer time and to bring their little games and occupations to one side of the table. They were "doll" girls with a strong leaning to paper dolls, the replenishing and enlargement of the wardrobes of these dolls was, as I remember it, their favorite amusement. The few remaining samples show quite an ingenuity in the designing of costumes, according to the latest fashion plates, apparently, the heads of these ladies and gentlemen were cut from some magazine and mounted on heavy paper and then suits and dresses of various colors and styles were cut to fit, with draperies and trains and sashes of different hues carefully pasted on, some elaborately decorated with a gold trim and huge puffed sleeves made by shirring thin pieces of paper and binding with a plain band. Each doll was named and many were the exciting adventures of these paper doll families. I can remember a distinct amusement at their pleasure -- I suppose from my lofty 8-year seniority and my complete lack of interest in such occupation for myself. Now, for the first time, as I gaze at the remains of their activity, I can see the imagination and creativeness involved.

It was to this table in the dining room that I brought my evening study until I was through high school. In later years of training, certain passages of Cicero or Caesar, a theorem in geometry or a scene in Macbeth always brought up a picture of this old room where I first met them.

One winter I became intensely interested in reading about Arctic explorations. Even now, any suggestion of expeditions to the frigid zones, a newspaper article or casual remark, transports me, not first to the poles, but to this little lamp-lit room, warm and cozy from the glowing fire in the airtight stove, and the two windows that looked out over snow piled sills to the unbroken expanse of the sleeping garden. The lamplight falls on the beautiful face of my mother with head bent over some task that would add to the comfort or joy of one of us. It falls on my father's stern face, his eyes fixed on his book, upon my sisters who were so alike that no one outside the family pretended to tell them apart.

My father would get up occasionally to feed the fire. If the opened door revealed a fine bed of coals, he reported the fact laconically. He was a man of few words. The remark was enough to send my sisters for the corn popper, corn and butter. There was always a trip to the cellar for apples which my father pared, quartered and divided equitably.

My father and mother had, as I have mentioned before, very strict standards. They did not need to use corporal punishment. They had their own ways and they were powerful. I had at one time, apparently become quite self-sufficient and a bit over-bearing in my imitation of the prevalent attitude of some school mates. I dashed into the house one day at noon, tossed a new botany book onto one chair and my hat on another, as I imitated the voices of my friends, loudly complaining, "There just is no use, I simply can't learn the stuff." My mother said not one word, simply looked at the two chairs I had just burdened and continued putting our dinner on the table. I quickly apologized for my carelessness and continued my tirade against botany, quoting Ruth and Etta frequently, knowing very well how much my mother disliked having me quote friends, rather than speaking my own thoughts.

At this moment, my father came in and in his quiet way remarked, "Botany should be very interesting. You will enjoy knowing the correct names for our friends in the woods." I turned my withering protest in his direction. "But you've no idea how hard the words are. Ruth says we could learn all this in the woods and not have to know all the names and even how they are spelled. Just look at this," and I produced my book and hunted for some name to impress him. "I'll just never remember them for two minutes. Here's 'lyrate' but I had to admit that it wasn't too hard since the leaf was shaped like a lyre. My father encouraged me to hunt further so I produced "spatulate, serrate, palmate, obcordate, saggitate," but for each one my father was able to challenge my mind with some familiar association. I was not going to admit defeat, however, and as I rose from the table to return to school, I reiterated my conviction that I could never learn it all.

My mother had kept very quiet during the conversation but at this last fling, her contribution was ready. She told me how very sad she was that I couldn't learn botany but she was very sure I could learn to keep house properly and that I might as well start learning right that minute. I couldn't quite believe what she intended but since there were still some minutes before the bell would ring I hurried to obey her instructions. She calmly criticized my method of clearing the table, pointing out that it required a mind as well as hands to do housework successfully. She was so deadly serious and when I could stand it no longer and feared I would be late for school, she reminded me that an education was costly in time and ability -- that they had hoped to give me an education so that I could be a teacher as I had planned to be, but that if I had discovered this early that there were subjects I could not learn, I would be much better off concentrating on housework which she was sure I could learn to do.

Well, my protestations and my promises and my assurances that I could learn all the hard words in my book, finally were sufficient and I was released. I wish I could run as fast today as I did on that memorable day as I dashed across fields and over fences in my zeal to gain the school's threshhold and start learning.

Several days later, my father presented me with two flowers he had found on a drive in the country. "See if you can find out what they are." "Do you know" was my answer as I took out my book to test my new knowledge. "Yes, but see for yourself." We sat down on the steps and I began the intensely interesting search. I scrutinized stamens, pistil and the large pink petals of one of them. After going over my material and the keys furnished in the text, I said, "If I have not made a mistake, this ought to be a marsh hibiscus, but I never heard of such a flower." "Well done, now try the other." This did not take quite as long for I had gained some confidence and I asked, "Could it be the blossom of the tulip tree?" Again I was right and my father's smile was worth a day's labor and no lecture could have been so effective.

Always an obedient child, I cannot at this distance explain how I happened to run away to go skating. On the way home, my puritan conscience called me to judgment. It was always the rule of our household that I should come straight home from school, unless previous arrangements had been made. This day I joined a group of girls to go skating.

It was dark when I ran the last few rods to the house. The family was at supper but I paid no attention to them but went into the kitchen and left my skates by the stove. When I stalked through the dining room, not daring to glance at the table for I was very hungry. As I passed my mother, I said, heroically, "I'm going right to bed without any supper." There was no need for an explanation for my mother understood that I was inflicting upon myself the severest punishment I knew. The matter was never mentioned. No wonder a spanking was not called for in such a conscience-dominated New England family.

I cannot leave the story of this little cottage without a word about my tiny room under the slanting roof and the pleasures therein. When we had company or on very cold nights in the winter, the parlor fire was lighted. There was a big drum in my room. For the present generation, it may be necessary to explain that a drum is a round or oval sheet iron affair through which the stove pipe coming up through the floor from below allows the last bit of heat to be utilized before the smoke goes into the chimney. On fireless nights, we children scudded through the cold parlors to the equally cold rooms, made short work of undressing and plunged deep into a bed with a temperature only slightly modified by a hot flatiron or brick wrapped in flannel.

Evenings when the room was warn, it became my sanctuary. It was my joy to draw the little table close to the drum and there revel in a new book discovered in the school library, or dream over a sheet of paper, pencil in hand. Here, just for the delight of doing were produced stories, poetry, sketches and what were called "essays." This fascination for writing has persisted, and a sheet of virgin paper always stirs the longing to write something on it, but it has not produced anything vitally important in the writing line.

In this little room, a journal was kept into which went my most secret emotions. I spent my hard-garnered savings for a case that locked. The journal was written, more or less regularly until I was 24 years old.

It must have been about this time that some of us conceived the idea of writing a school paper. Anything that had to do with writing caught my attention at once and I went into the project with energy as most of the work devolved on me. The little magazine was much like others of its class, containing stories, poems, locals and jokes when we could think of any, and an occasional illustration. It was written in double columned pages on foolscap, in imitation of a paper called, "The Little Corporal" which was popular at that time. We named ours "The Little Captain." To my knowledge no copy survives. If one existed it would make a sorry showing by the side of Lewis Carroll's "The Rectory Umbrella" and "Mischamasch."

As I think back over those years in Dowagiac in the late 1860's and early '70's, I am impressed over the utter simplicity and wholesomeness of life in this small midwestern community, typical of many such towns scattered over this country. We were free to wander over meadows and woods as far as our legs would carry us, to gather wild flowers and nuts by the bushel. I'm afraid that conservation was not resting heavily on our minds, but I do remember the reverence we had for what we had gathered. Horse chestnuts were collected avidly but I do not recall what we did with them.

Skating and sledding were major occupations during the harsh winters and the long summer hours were devoted to amateur dramatics and croquet.

This was a serious game enjoyed by all ages and I can well remember my anger one time because I suspected our minister, Mr. Harmon (A.G. Harmon Universalist Church minister), of letting me win. That was one thing I could not abide. I was a hard player at whatever I tried but I did passionately want to fight my own way.

Many were the arguments I had with the umpire over our games of baseball, my favorite sport and one in which I excelled. To this day I cannot resist a good game even when I have to be satisfied with a radio version. In my mind I can see every play and have devised a chart to record a record of each play.

Church suppers were a delight to all of us. Here, small children and big, parents, grandparents, and all the citizens of the community would gather. Such feasts as the women of the church prepared. What agony for fear you might not get to the "first serving." To wait was unbearable. The supper was always followed by entertainments of various kinds -- home-grown, naturally-group games, fortune telling and singing. Here was the center for fellowship and fun.

Box socials were also held. Lunch boxes were prepared and elaborately decorated by the women of the church, and by the girls. Each one was done with the maker's own touch. These were auctioned off to the highest bidder. Certain cooks were well known for their ability so much intrigue was involved in trying to find out which boxes had been prepared by them. Since the one who bought the box was entitled to share it with its maker, the younger set used a different standard -- the popularity of the girl far outweighed the risk of what was in the box and many were the tricks and maneuvers and signals used to solve the mystery.

There were many attempts at the earning of a few pennies by various means, but the outstanding example of the budding business man was our popcorn boy, who built up quite a business for himself and later sold newspapers in Grand Rapids, taught himself law, and became a United States Senator from the State of Michigan, William Alden Smith.

As for the school work itself, at the time of my high school years, the course was very simple. Graduation did not mean any such education as falls to the lot of the high school student today, although many of us were inspired to know the joy of reading good books. I do not remember that we had separate courses although some took Latin and some did not. The Latin was poor and there was little of it. We read one book of Caesar and three orations of Cicero. To this was added a little algebra, very little, plane geometry, fairly good work in English, general history and one term of German.

A year later both ancient and modern languages were deleted from the course, much to the indignation of some of the parents. From some one came a love for books and writing and I managed to be awarded a dictionary for some accomplishment along these lines. My yearning for knowledge was insatiable and the school library as well as private ones offered to me, were eagerly visited and the books read avidly.

The week before Commencement was devoted to public examinations and these ordeals were attended by townspeople, students and alumni. It sounds very cruel now to contemplate, but as I look back, I believe we simply accepted this final examination period as part of the expected routine of life. For any student to fail in such a public manner would have been a catastrophe.

There were only three in my graduating class and on that day I was offered a contract to teach the lowest grade in the public schools for the following term, for the princely sum of $320 for the year. To me, it was a princely sum. So at the age of sixteen, I was started on a teaching career that was to last for forty-four years in the State of Michigan.

In this age of specialization when of every teacher is demanded a college education, including many hours devoted to courses in education, itself, it may be interesting to look back to the day when some of us entered the profession with very little equipment indeed.

Nothing but the courage of youth and the audacity of inexperience could have made me venture into that room with 84 little children, half of whom had never been in school before. But some guardian angel must have stood over me throughout the year, for at its close, the board, instead of turning me out. promoted me with the higher class into the next room.

During these months of teaching, all my leisure time was spent in study. I was hungry for knowledge and eagerly seized every opportunity offered. From somewhere came the inspiration to learn Greek, but it was not taught in the school and the little town did not boast of many who knew anything of it. At last I found a minister who had learned Greek 40 years before but still retained a scholarly love for it and he consented to give me a start, with semi-occasional lessons. I plunged into its drudgery with pure delight. The results were not astonishing but it was a valuable lesson in study habits.

By the spring of my second year of teaching, I had saved enough money for a few months of school. I was poor but I was ambitious and I was hungry for an education. I had heard of a small school that was very cheap, supported by the Universalist Church, and not very far away, so in April of 1874, I ventured to Smithson College in Logansport, Ind.

One of the few "out of school" activities that I remember is an amateur production of "Uncle Tom's Cabin." In those days every town, hamlet or city witnessed some kind of a production of it. Road companies traveled the circuit throughout the width and breadth of the northern states, performing in opera houses, town halls and tents. There seemed to be no end to the interest which lasted more than forty years.

In the year of 1873 a home-spun production was planned. I had my heart set on taking the part of Topsy but it was decided that it would not be quite dignified for a school teacher to take such a part so I had to be satisfied with Miss Ophelia.

(It is believed this autobiography was written sometime in the 1920's after Mrs. Milner had retired. She wrote much more covering all her years of teaching experience.)

59

Frances Willard

Miss Frances Willard, president of the National WCTU, and widely known throughout the country, was in Dowagiac on December 11, 1887.

Even though she made an excellent impression on local citizens, it was a long time before Dowagiac could be convinced to vote dry. An account of her visit here appeared in The Dowagiac Republican of December 15, 1887.

"Miss Frances Willard, president of the National Women's Christian Temperance Union, spoke to an audience of 800 to 1,000 in this city at the opera house Sunday evening on the subject of temperance.

"Her reputation as a platform speaker suffered no setback with her audience on Sunday. It seems to be the unanimous opinion of all who heard her that the manner in which she handled her subject was calculated to advance the cause of temperance tenfold more tnan that of the average lecturer.

"She has a remarkably fine voice and it seemed to be no effort for her to make herself distinctly heard all over the house. The best of attention was given her throughout. The local union are deserving of the gratitude of our citizens for this rare treat."

"Miss Willard occupied the pulpit at the Methodist Church Sunday morning and deliver a very elegant sermon to a large congregation."

60

Doctor McMaster

The late Dr. H.S. McMaster, who came to Dowagiac in 1871, described in later years what the village was like in those days. The house torn down at 101 West Division Street was the old McMaster home and office.

He said that from Decatur "he came over Henderson Hill in the evening. There being then no system of street lighting he could see only here and there a light in a window. Crossing the railroad at the upper crossing and coming down West Railroad Street he passed a small house on what is now the Heddon company property, then owned and occupied by a Mr. Perkins." George Whitmore house stood nearby and the space between that and Oak Street was occupied by his sheds, barns and drays.

Dr. McMaster said that by the census taken the year before Dowagiac had 2,074 people, with their houses all well fenced to keep out the 60 to 100 cows and cattle, about half with bells on, and numerous hogs, geese and chickens.

All of Brooklyn, later called the Hopkins addition, over the present vaiduct, and many other considerable tracts of land about the town were in commons and with the street and vacant lots afford ample pasturage for all this stock, while the west end, then called "Shanty Town," was an extensive goose pasture.

None of the streets or the roads leading into town had been gravelled and the road across the swamp north of town was rough corduroy, dangerous both to horses and vehicles.

The old red depot was still in use. The schools were the old

Central School with five rooms, and the Ward School with three rooms.

Dr. T.G. Rix and his brother, John, were the only dentists and occupied an office upstairs at the northwest corner of Front and Commercial Streets.

The physicians in 1871 were Drs. C.W. Morse, C.P. Prindle, C.J. Curtis, L.V. Rouse, P.I. Mulvane, J.H. Wheeler, G.W. Fosdick, S.S. Stebbins, E.B. Reed and Dr. McMaster, ten in all.

"A little later the number was increased by Drs. Sherwood and Marr," said Dr. McMaster, and "so that with four or five students who sometimes prescribed in busy times, we had at least one time, 14 doctors and all very busy through many months of the year."

61

Abner Moon

This community should be forever indebted to Abner Mack Moon, who throughout his long life, gathered up pioineer history and published it, as he was a long time newspaper writer and publisher. He was born on a farm in Porter Township, Van Buren County, in 1849. As a boy he grew up among the Potawatomi Indians and who were his playmates.

He early learned the Potawatomi language and all of his life remained proficient in it. Most of his life was spent in Dowagiac, and in time he knew the name of every Indian for miles around, the names of their wives and of their children. His son, the late Don Moon, who used to accompany his father on trips out in the country, could remember his father hailing Indians he would meet, all speaking Potawatomi to him. At one time he acted as agent of the Potwatomi band in attempting to get them repaid for lands the government had taken from them.

In his early days he was associated with Richard and James Heddon in publishing beekeeping journals. He was connected with a beekeepers' magazine in New York City for a brief period and in Indianapolis, and later went to Rome. Georgia where he and his father published Moon's Bee Journal for four years.

But it was as a newspaper man he was best known. He first published the Lawton Tribune for one year. In 1876 he started The Marcellus News which he published for four years, and then coming to Dowagiac in 1881 to purchase The Dowagiac Times.

He was on the staff of The Dowagiac Daily News from time to

time; published the old Dowagiac Herald; Moon's Weekly, and with his son, Don, the old Cassopolis Democrat.

During all these years, it was his custom to go out and interview pioneers and record what they had to tell about the early days in the community, and some of these stories are contained in this book.

The late Harry H. Whiteley, one of his staunch admirers, used to relate how Ab Moon operated. He had a fund of stories, which he would rewrite and polish up from time to time. He used an old double decked typewriter, lower case on the lower deck and the upper case or caps on the upper deck. He refused to let Mr. Whiteley buy him a new typewriter, he was used to the old one. Some of the keys were broken off and after he had finished writing, would take his copy and fill in all the missing letters.

The Dowagiac Creek was never referred to in his stories other than "The Raging Dowagiac"; and "The rolling hills of Newberg", and "Plutocratic Porter", were among his designations.

He was an active Democrat, was postmaster of Dowagiac for several years, justice of the peace for many years, and at one time, county drain commissioner. He also served as Dowagiac city clerk. Although a Democrat he was also at one time on the staff of The Dowagiac Republican, in the days when politics were most partisan, which testifies as to his ability as a newspaperman.

62

Abner Moon Stories

The late Webb Miller, whose name tops the list of newspapermen in the Overseas Club in New York City, believed that Abner Moon could have been famous had he received proper publicity. Miller, a graduate of Dowagiac High School, came home for a rare visit shortly before World War II and stopped at The Daily News where he had gained his first experience writing sports news. He asked me if I would save Ab Moon stories when I ran across any in the old files, which I agreed to do.

Webb Miller who was the UP European manager, had just written a book, "I Found No Peace," predicting the coming war. I never was able to save the stories for him, for he was killed in a fall from a train in London where he lived.

Following are several examples of Ab Moon's gentle humor:

Careless Hunter

The danger resulting from careless shooting on the part of hunters was emphasized yesterday when Oswald Peebles, a farmer south of town, received a bullet wound in his left shoulder while plowing corn. To his surprise Mr. Peebles heard no report of a gun, but he could judge from which direction the bullet came.

Investigation showed that a hunter from Dailey, had the day before, passed by the Peebles farm and had fired a shot from his rifle into a signboard. The bullet had struck a knot and did not work through until yesterday, when it went on, and Mr. Peebles being in range of the singboard, it hit him. Had Mr. Beebles been a tall man the wound might have been fatal.

This is the first accident of this kind reported this year.

A Strange Noise

POKAGON — Residents of Pokagon were greatly mystified Saturday by a strange noise which passed over the village about noon in a southerly direction. Several theories were advanced as to the cause of the peculiar visitor, but it remained for Hamilton Hostetter, a local dry goods dealer, to solve the mystery.

Mr. Hostetter had been to the creek after a pail of water, and saw the sound as it passed over. He says it was about 40 feet long, and as large around as a stovepipe. It had a hole in one side, indicating that it had struck a treetop somewhere. Mr. Hostetter believes that the sound came from some factory whistle and was probably jerked from the whistle by the high wind and was never heard in its home town.

Mr. Hostetter said it disappeared in the direction of Niles, and he thinks that unless it struck something head on it would last for two or three days.

As evidence that all our citizens did not accept Mr. Hostetter's explanation it was noticed that there was a larger attendance at church here yesterday than usual.

March 31, 1916 -- What is supposed to have been a meteor fell in the middle of Dewey Lake last night at about 10 o'clock, making a tremendous noise and lighting up the sky.

Investigation this forenoon by Epsom Baxter and others revealed the hole in the water where the strange visitor struck it, but if there was any meteor there it was buried in the mud out of sight. The water was slightly muddy however.

The circumstance will be featured here the coming summer with a view to bringing resorters here. A photograph of the hole taken by Truman Miles, owner of one of the chief resorts, will be used for advertising. Nothing of the kind ever happened here before.

Realist Art

DAILEY — April 18, 1916 - The remarkable genius of Joshua Tripe, our village sign painter, may result in a suit for damages being brought against the village. Mr. Tripe a few days ago completed a correspondence school course in sign painting, and to show his skill, painted a board fence on the side of a barn, standing along the main street.

It looked so natural that several farmers have skinned their knuckles trying to hitch their teams to it, and even birds have attempted to light on it, slipping down the side of the barn to the ground and flying away disgusted.

The climax came Friday, however, when Tripe's bulldog chased a stranger down the street, who in trying to get away attempted to jump the supposed fence and nearly knocked his brains out.

Several attorneys have already written the stranger, who gives his name as Frellinghusen, offering legal aid in getting damages out of either Tripe of the village, it has not been decided which.

A Snake Warning

June 15, 1916 - Elnathan Plung of this city had a thrilling experience yesterday with a monster rattlesnake, which had come out of the jungle on the Indian Lake pike (M-61 west) near the iron bridge to sun itself, and which Mr. Plung in his excitement, drove over with his car.

As the left fore wheel of the car struck the snake the snake curled around it and bit it several times before its life was crushed out. Almost immediately the wheel began to swell, and it was with difficulty that Mr. Plung got to town, the wheel being so large that it would have made the car run around in a circle but for his heroic efforts to keep it in the track. No such experience was ever had here before.

The heavy rains have driven the snakes out of the swamps this year and they have been quite plentiful on the uplands and in the highways. Autoists will do well to turn out for them.

63

Simon Pokagon

There is one little story that occured outside the city limits I want to include which concerns Simon Pokagon, who headed the Potawatomi Indians of this area many years ago. Simon, a brilliant, well educated man, became so well known that school children of Chicago saved their pennies to have a statue erected in a park (Grant Park I believe) of Simon Pokagon. He died near Hartford about 1898 or 1899.

Not long before his death he visited his birthplace near Sumnerville in company with his long time friend, Abner Moon. Moon, who had at one time been an agent for the Potawatomi Indians in this area, and Pokagon were talking about the troubles of the Indians when Pokagon remarked:

"It would have been better if my ancestors had killed Columbus and his men when they landed," explaining that the Indian would have been spared all his subsequent troubles with the white race.

64

Dowagiac's Biggest Man

Back in the 1880's lived Dowagiac's biggest man, Cor "Fatty" Brownell. No one ever knew how much he weighed. At least three people told me about him, Cecile Mosher, George Chapman and Attorney "Deac" ReShore. They estimated he weighed at least 450 pounds.

The late George Chapman had a couple of stories to tell about him. Brownell was night baggageman for the then Michigan Central Railroad. One of his duties was to take care of the switch lights, light them or put them out as the case might be.

One night he started down the track with a lantern in each hand. Because of his tremendous width, those lanterns were spread pretty far apart. A freight train coming into the local station came to a jarring halt, the engineer being positive that he saw another freight train backing up.

It wasn't -- it was Fatty Brownell coming down the track with his two lanterns. The freight train crew was pretty burned up at what was a natural mistake on their part.

Another story told about him by Chapman is that once when he wanted to see the circus, he hired Perry Conklin and his express wagon to take him out to the circus grounds. He couldn't sit in the front seat with Perry, he was too large. His tremendous bulk filled the back end of the express wagon.

Don ReShore told this: Fatty was very fond of custard and never could have enough to suit his tremendous appetite. His mother resolved that for once he was going to have enough and she set to work and made him a whole tub of custard. It was a small tub to be sure but he ate it all and then rolled around the yard in agony for half the night -- but for once he had had enough custard.

Cecile Mosher as a child remembered him and recalled that he carried his lunch in a big market basket and it was full of lunch.

She also said that in spite of his tremendous size he was an expert skater. He loved to dance and in spite of his size was light on his feet.

No doubt there are other stories about him but these are all I had.

65

Stephen Topash

In the early days the Potawatomi Indians lived mainly in Silver Creek and not in Dowagiac with perhaps one or two exceptions. But many were well known here, and the names of Topash, Motay, Weesaw, Winchester, Morseau, Hamilton, Augusta, Pokagon, Cushway and others were familiar to Dowagiac residents.

It is noted that "palefaces" who grew up with the Indians in their childhood, have nearly always remained firm friends and that was true with many.

One Indian who was remembered for years in Dowagiac was Stephen Topash. He was a friend of the late Attorney James H. Kinnane who had a high regard for him, who said that Topash always kept his word. He was meticulous in financial matters, and if he borrowed money, could be depended upon to repay it "on the dot." He was a man of tremendous strength said Kinnane and not many cared to tangle with him.

In an article written about him years ago, it stated he was born near Warsaw, Ind. and came to Cass County with his parents when two years old; that his grandmother was a daughter of Topinabee and through his mother's line, was related to the Pokagons. The family settled on a 40-acre farm in Silver Creek later owned by Andrew Downey. When the government forced the Indians to move to Kansas, his mother hid her children in the woods, and from there went to Pipestone Township to stay with friends.

"Stephen Topash grew up in the forest. He learned how to cure his people bitten by the deadly moccasin, how to cure many diseases the flesh is heir to, including ivy and sumac poisoning. He learned how to trap the otter and the fox, how to lure the deer to its death, and how to make the furs into garments.

"As he grew into manhood -- and he did grow, 6 feet, 2½ inches tall -- he took his place in the fields, and few could equal him. It is said that in the early '70's himself and his brother, Joeta, in two days cut 30 acres of wheat for G.I. Sherman in Keeler -- 7½ acres per day, and he could cut five cords of two-foot wood in a day at anytime."

His marriage to Angeline Rail, "a devout woman, good housewife, and a spendid singer," took place in 1883. They never had any children, but lived long and happily together.

It was said there are many buildings in Dowagiac framed by timbers hewn "by this stalwart Indian."

Today more Indians live within the city limits of Dowagiac than they ever did in Stephen Topash's day. In recent years they have banded together and organized themselves to protect and maintain their ancient heritage of which they are justly proud.

66

That Other Side

People who knew I was doing this book gave been nudging me to write about another phase of Dowagiac history not seen in print. At first I said, "no way, " but it was old fashioned sin and people today would hardly give it a second thought. One person even offered to share a family scandal with me. I plan to stay on the edge of things so to speak and name no names.

At one time Dowagiac was said to have had 16 saloons, which didn't seem to leave much room for anything else. By 1899, according to the Dowagiac directory, state law had reduced the number to 10 and remained that way until the county finally went dry.

That took a lot of doing. Although for years the rest of the county was voting "dry," Dowagiac was able to overcome that sentiment with the help of various "wet" allies in other parts of the county.

All saloons were in the business district and as a child I marched in local option parades and sang temperance songs in front of the bars. I can remember how the smell of beer pervaded Front Street in the summer, and occasionally seeing a drunk roll out into the street from behind those swinging doors. Among the earliest saloons were the Blue Ruin on the north side or Beeson Street and the Red Ruin directly across the street. Eventually the city was able to muster up a dry majority.

Van Buren County was dry for years and its thirsty citizens had to visit Berrien or Cass Counties. In those days at least 20 trains a day passed through here many of them stopping. There was one

215

eastbound train that stopped at midnight and was known as the "Saturday Night Drunk Special," usually loaded with inebriated Decatur citzens.

The late Dr. Willis Dunbar of Western Michigan University, a native of Hartford, said the same thing happened in his town, only Hartfordites' trains took them to Berrien County.

Saturday nights were big nights, the streets were crowded with people paying their bills and doing their shopping, while others were quenching their thirst. There were always a number of fights and the city marshal usually wrestled the combatants off to jail to cool off.

For years right down town there existed a "house," which may not have equalled the best little one in Texas, but it was notorious for miles around. I thought if Webb Miller could write about it in his book, "I Found No Peace," I could too.

According to local legends some of the city fathers were too "involved" to be able to close the place down. And there are stories about this too.

One time the madam, it was reported, bought up all the seats in the dress circle for a famous stage play that was being presented at the Beckwith Theater. Then she and her girls, all dressed in silks and satins, paraded sown the aisle to their seats, much to the amazement and secret delight of some of the other patrons.

Webb Miller, who later became a famous United Press correspondent, in the beginning of his book, told how he and another high school classmate decided they were men enough to visit the house too. The madam thought otherwise and shooed them back down stairs.

It was said that a mayor, who had not been a "guest" there, closed the place, while others said she got religion. At any rate she never became so completely reformed, but ran a speakeasy here during prohibition days. When Webb paid his last visit to Dowagiac shortly before his untimely death in London, he stopped in at The Daily News office. I had just read his book and was able to tell him she was still alive and well and living in Dowagiac. Webb looked stunned, clapped his hands to his head and said, "My God, I had better leave town."

We had a pretty seamy area in Dowagiac for many years. It had to be seen to be believed, I know, I saw it just once. But that has changed too.

Chicago and Detroit newspapers made much of the happenings in Dowagiac and helped to give it a reputation it might not otherwise have had. But as I said, it was not a typical small town.

67

How It Was

In this final chapter I am telling a little of how it was "in the olden days" of newspapering. I really enjoyed my years as a newspaper woman. I do not use the word "journalist" it was considered a bad word in my day. I have worked with so many fine people and my editors allowed me a lot of leeway.

I have been fortunate enough to live in entirely different eras and for this reason I am including a portion of the story I wrote at the time I completely retired from The Daily News on September 1, 1977. However I still keep one foot in the door with contributions to the Cook Book edition. The Daily News was a most important part of my life for over 45 years and I would like to recall and preserve some of those earlier days, describing an era in Dowagiac now gone.

At the time I wrote this article (1977) I could only touch on some of the highlights of my years on the paper. I will quote from it as follows:

"We started in the days of hot lead, followed by offset and only this year to computerized typewriters. We never dreamed we would become our own printers.

"Today we work with a generation that has never seen a type louse and never will. A chace, stone, galley, font and proof press are unknown to them.

"We worked temporarily during the summer of 1928. That was the year the interurban stopped running between Dowagiac, Indian Lake, Eau Claire, Benton Harbor and St. Joe. When we returned for good in 1929 we took over circulation and classifieds and during the depression added proof reading.

"The paper published six days a week and the office used to be open those six days until 5:30 p.m. In 1934 we were transferred to the news department and we really put in long hours. We wound down to two days a week in 1970 but put in a lot of mileage on our typewriter at home.

"When we first began work the Roaring Twenties were still roaring. Dowagiac was not and never has been a typical small town and roared right along with the rest, a little ahead of most of them. We knew where all the speakeasies were for miles and cellars were for making home brew.

"We could go anywhere by train; cars had running boards and rumble seats; everyone was learning the Charleston and young males carried hip flasks to dances. Politics were always lively in Dowagiac, with occasional quiet intervals, but "The Pink Sheet" kept things pretty well stirred up.

"We had brick pavements, three movies, beautiful ornamental street lights, Postal Telegraph, Western Union, A & P and Kroger stores. Dowagiac was "The Furnace City of America" with the Round Aok, Rudy, Premier and Steel Furnace companies. Of all the manufacturing companies then, only Heddon's survives today.

"The Community State Bank building and lot now occupies the site where The Daily News held forth for so long. When we started work Morgan Finch's tire and battery shop occupied the corner lot adjoining The Daily News on the east, Charley White's automobile agency and garage were on the west, and now a part of the Community State Bank building."

(The Daily News in the late 1960's moved to the former Round Oak factory office on Spaulding Street where it is today.)

Pete Potter's blacksmith shop was directly behind The Daily News on Penn Avenue. And across the street was Charley Hubbard's livery stable. There was another blacksmith shop on Penn Avenue between West Division and Commercial shaded by a huge elm tree. On hot summer afternoons the ring of the anvil would echo through our office. Also on Commercial were Blackmond's Jewelry store, Solf's Bakery, Redner's Grocery and the Lee State Bank on the corner opposite Is. Oppenheim's store.

I can shut my eyes and walk into the old Daily News Office up those three steps and see everything the way it was, the UP (now UPI) machines chattering in the printer room, Harry H. Whiteley. owner and publisher at his desk in the corner. John Coller was editor and he and Maurine Lamoreaux were the entire news staff.

Fred McKenzie comprised the entire display advertising department and worked at least 60 hours a week. Alice Biek and Mary Woodruff made up the rest of the office staff.

In the back room Tom Taylor was foreman assisted by Leonard Bright. Sitting at the linotypes were Kate Bigelow, Matt Amersdorfer and Don Moon. Jim McKenzie was pressman and Ethel Brown the proof reader, a job I later inherited from her. Homer Pompey fired the big Round Oak furnace and kept the place in order.

There were 10 newsboys (no girls in those days). Among them were Lawrence Carey, Hal Palmer, Tom Mosier, Dick Hunsberger and Mike Bobik.

Things were booming until the stock market crash in October, 1929 and after awhile we began to feel the effects of the depression. There was no such thing as unemployment benefits or Social Security, in fact there was nothing to protect the worker. The Daily News managed to weather it but it was rough going.

Probably our most traumatic experiences were during World War II. I had started a Service column which contained news of service men and letters from them. It became a daily affair and soon The Daily News went all over the world. I have had boys tell me they have had it delivered in fox holes. I shared the grief of many of the parents who lost sons, and in time also suffered the terrible anxiety of knowing my own son was in the thick of the fighting.

Anything that happened in the community I wrote about it. I covered county board meetings, school board meetings and in time the college board. In fact I was present at the meeting when it was "born."

When I started there was no local radio and no TV and our only communciation through the air was the telephone. But newspapers not only have survived the competition but are gaining.

How good the people in the community have been to me and I cannot begin to name them all. There are literally hundreds of them.

In 1934 when Maurine Lamoreaux left, I took her place, still only two of us in the news department. Mae Rosemeier took my place as proof reader, and when she retired the same week I did, she had been the bookkeeper for many years.

One of my duties was to do the "Looking Back" column and this really sparked my interest in local history. It wasn't hard, one great-great-grandfather had come to Cass County in 1828 as Penn Township's first white settler, and another great-great-grandfather came in 1829. My English great-grandparents came in the 1840's to Porter township and Carter Lake is named for them.

The first great-great-grandfather moved on to pioneer in Kalamazoo County in a year or two and is immortalized in a painting hanging in the Kalamazoo Museum as the first defendant in a trial in that county. He paid a $10 fine on an assault and battery charge. Thanks to Alexis Praus I have postcard pictures showing him surrounded by his dogs and Indian friends.

The late Harry H. Whiteley, owner and publisher for 40 years, suggested that I write a column about things going on in and around town and we named it "Down Town." I owe so much to him.

And the things that passed through that column, over 10,000 of them. All I can say is that nothing was sacred, I always found a place or an excuse for everything. Lots of little news items were carried there, even one special wedding. I helped along "feuds" among the local fishermen, I always liked to keep things stirred up and I had lots of help. And of course all the birthdays, that was a daily thing too. And my Christmas Birthday Club which was always very special; those funny letters from Beacher; often historical bits; and naturally, things about my beloved grandchildren.

People tell me they miss my column -- but let me tell you -- I miss you too.

INDEX

A

Adams & Hopkins, 34
Adams, Thos. W., 88
Agnew, H. E., 44
Alliger, Will, 123
Amersdorfer, Matt, 220
Amersdorfer & Wiltse, 137,
188
Alhambra Saloon, 35
Andrew, J.C., Geo., 33,34,39
Andrews, 121
Anderson, Mary, 54
Anderson, Dr. Wm., 129,130
Angle, Philip, 146
Anthony, Susan B., 29,54
Atwell, Freeman, 15,87
Atwell, Mrs. F. J., 99
Atwood, James, 72
Atwood, Louis, 185
Atwood, Wells, 33
Augusta, 213

B

Babbitt, 34
Bacon, Elizabeth, 144
Bailey, Jerusha E., 99
Balch, Arad C., 32,150
Baldwin, William, 114
Ball, Chester, 136
Ballengee, 33,88
Barber, John D., 39
Barnard, Chas. N., 101,104
Barney, Clarissa, 185

Barney, John, 185
Barney, Sarah, 96
Barney, William, 85
Bayes, Nora, 56
Beach, Daniel, 68
Beach, O. G., 59
Beach, Harrison, 221
Beals, Dr., 188
Becraft, J. O., 44,167
Becraft, Isaiah, 88, 106
Beckwith, Della, 68,96
Beckwith, Kate, 61,62
Beckwith, Mrs. P. D.,99
Beckwith, Philo D., 19,41,54,
58,60,68,70,100,108,122,145
Beckwith, Stephen 68
Beckwith, Walter G., 43,144
Bedford, Martha, 96
Beery Pharmacy, 15
Beeson, Jacob, 14,31,33
Beeson, Jesse G., 43
Bennett, Mrs. Geo., 136,137
Benson, Sam, 123
Bernhardt, Sarah, 54,56
Bigelow, Charles, 45
Bigelow, Herman, 115
Bigelow, Hervey, 102,115
Bigelow, Kate, 220
Bigelow, Otis, 116
Biek, Alice, 220
Bilderback, John, 145
Bird, Ella, 96
Blackmond, Fred, 108,126
Blackmond, Steve, 127
Blue Ruin Saloon, 27
Bobik, Mike, 220
Bock, Henry, 163,176
Bock, Nicholas, 15,17,34,157,
158

Bolduc, Robert, 45
Bowling, Benjamin, 115
Bowling, Mrs. H. D., 99
Bowling, Thomas, 187
Brace, Charles Loring, 118
Bradbury, Juliet, 94
Bradon, Dr., 188
Brady, Dave, 114
Brayton, Dr., 35
Breece, Anna, 96
Bright, Leonard, 220
Brizendine, Frances, 17
Brown, Ed, 109
Brown, Ethel, 220
Brown, Sidney Smith, 97
Brownell, Cor, 211
Brownell, Ira, 102
Buck, Marcia, 96
Buell, Mary, 86
Buffington, H. C. 43
Burling, Robert Gill, 135
Bull, Ole, 84
Burlingame (Ray), 19
Burnside, General, 142
Burrows, J. C., 41
Byrnes, John, 174

C

Cady, Nellie, 96
Campbell, Bob, 137
Campbell, Malcolm, 49,151
Campbell, W. H., 43,137,143
Cappou, Father John, 98
Carlisle, Mr., 38
Carney, Dee, 49
Carreno, Theresa, 84
Carey, Lawrence, 220
Carver, Ella, 96
Chandler, Zack, 41
Chapman, George, 57,211
Chappell, Mrs. E. C., 99
Chappell, Enos, 145,146
Chappell, Guy, 146
Cheesborough, Miss, 86
Cheesborough, Nicholas, 14,
28

Choate, N. F., 72
Clarke, Ada, 187
Clarke Brothers, 148,149
Clarke, C. Fred, 72
Clarke, Julian, 149
Clarke, Joseph, 16,57,141,148,
169
Clarke, William, 188
Clark, Wayne, 104
Clisbee, Charles W., 142
Clymer, Floyd, 49
Cobb, Irvin S., 78
Coffinger, A. W., 111
Coghlan, Rose, 56
Codding, William, 134
Colburn, William, 134
Colby, Eleanor, 179
Colby, Gilbert, 19
Colby, Horace, 19,94,179
Coller, John, 220
Compton, Hannah, 86
Conklin, William, 170
Conkling, Warren, 88
Cook, Russell, 52
Cooper, Benjamin, 17,34
Copley, Miss, 86
Crawford, John, 71
Crawford, Richard, 146
Crippen, George, 116
Crowell, William, 138,140
Cross, Isaac, 188
Cullom, Maggie, 96
Cullom, Mary, 96
Cullom, Sadie, 185
Curtis, Dr. C. J., 204
Curtis, Lillie A., 99
Curtis, R. E., 44
Cushman, Florence, 99,189
Custer, Gen. George A., 144
Cutter, John F., Sr. 102,104

D

Davis, 60
Davis, Bob, 75
Davis, Jefferson, 143
Day, Lucian, 134
Deal, Owen, 158

INDEX

Defendorf, Flavia, 184,187
Defendorf, Harmon, 116
Defoe, Nat, 134,164
Denman, H. B., 150
Dennison, R. C., 106,141
Dewey, B. L., 72,88
DeWitt, Isaac, 146
Deyo, Mr., 142
Dickson, Mrs. Lurany, 99
Dillman, Hiram, 163
Doolittle, S. C. 108
Dopp, Mathew B., 146
Doster, James S., 85
Douglas Brigade, 133
Downey, Andrew, 133
Drury, Miss, 172,173
Dunbar, Dr. Willis, 216
Dunning, Isaac R., 94
Dunning, O. B., 94
Dunnington, Fred, 50

E

Edwards, J. R., 158
Edwards, Lewis, 85
Edwards, W. C., 108
Elkerton Hotel, 107
Elliot, George, 54
Elliott, Ray, 178
Ellis, Amelia, 96
Ellsworth, Andrew, 146
Emmons, John K., 165

F

Felt, Laura, 96
Farr, Willis M., 50
Fiero, Abram, 138,139
Finch, Clark, 50
Finch, Morgan, 219
Fletcher, Bevvie, 96
Fosdick Dr. George, 19,188, 200
Fowle, C. L., 72
Fox, George, 11,21,22,159

Frohman, Daniel, 56
Fraser, Annie, 96
Fry, Annette Riley, 117,120
Fuller, Louisa, 87

G

Gage, Benjamin, 160
Gage, Ebenezer, 70,85
Gage, Justus, 18,20,25,43,58, 85,91,94,150,157,159,175
Gage, John S., 70
Gage, Matilda Tinkler, 160
Gage, Wm. Harrison, 160
Gage, DeWitt, 160
Gantt, James L., 43,143
Gantt, S. N., 141
Gard, Brookfield, 167
Gardner, Archie, 52,55,104
Gardner, Charles, 68
Gardner, Jack, 61,104
Gardner, Jeff, 114,188
Garvey, M. T., 33,122
Genung, George, 108
Gerding, Carl, 34
Gillette, Fanny Camp, 178, 183
Gillette, Mrs. Clarence, 126
Gillette, John, 126,128
Gillette, George, 178
Gillette, KIng, 178-182
Gillette, Mott, 182,183
Gibbs, Gideon, 33,72,88,94, 106
Gough, John B., 84
Gould, Benjamin, 84
Greenleaf, C. J., 43
Greenleaf, Mrs. C.J., 150
Green, George W., 88
Greenwood, Grace, 16,169
Grush, John, 146

H

Hager, Sgt. Phneas E., 130

INDEX

Hain, Harold, Sylvia, 37,155
Hale, Dr., 188
Hall, George, 47
Hall, Jehial, 134
Hallock, Maria, 96
Hamilton, Abel, 163,165
Hamilton, Geo., Eliz., 163
Hamilton (Indian), 213
Hamilton, Patrick, 33,88,97, 161,163,175
Hannan, Chas., Will, 174
Hannan, Peter, 17,104
Harden, Mrs. F. L., 17
Harder's Brewery, 188
Harley, James, 179,182-83
Harmon, A. G., 198
Harris, Cecil, 57
Harris, Josie, 96
Harris, Paul, 57
Hart, William S., 55
Harter, Virgil, 116
Hastings, Chas., Eva, 80
Hebron, Fannie, Jane, Lydia, 96
Heddon, Charles, 78,79,80
Heddon, James, 19,44,71,75,79
Heddon, Richard, 72,76,79
Heddon, Will, 46,80,81
Hendrick, Isaac, 72
Hendryx, Coy, 173
Henwood, Bros., Edw., James, John, Richard, William, 145
Henwood, Thomas, 108,145
Herkimer, Sarah J., 126
Herold, Michael, 124
Higgins, George, 134
Hills, Mrs. Henry C., 87
Hills, Lottie, 94
Hirsch, Jacob, 33
Hollister, N.B., 33,150
Holmes, George, 108
Holmes, Richard, 43,58
Hoover, John, 134
Hopkins Addition, 203
Hotchkiss, Lucinda, 87
Howard, William G., 100
Howell, Silas, 164
Houser, Henry, 85

Hoyt, William F., 72,74
Hubbard, Charles, 219
Huff, Ashur, 134
Huff, Daniel 104
Huleminsky, 150
Hunsberger, Dick, 220
Huntington, Asa, 33,137,184, 185

I

Indian Trails, Villages, 22
Ingersoll, Addie, 88,171
Ingersoll, Robert, 55
Ingling, Samuel, 72

J

James, Frank, 115
James, Lewis, 146
Jarvis, Burton, 163
Jarvis, Norman, 138,163
Jarvis, Zadok, 163
Jessco, Co., 62
Jewell, E. Barlow, 108
Jewell, Stella, 96
Johnson, Mr., Mrs. Irving, 84
Johnson, Jesse, 103,104
Johnson, Philip, 77
Johnson, Mrs. Samuel, 99
Jones, Amanda, 99
Jones, Azro & Horace, 33
Jones, Frank, 131
Jones, Gilman, 33,88,141
Jones, Mrs. Gilman, 99
Jones, H. B., 43
Jones, Horace, 17
Jones, Lyle & Walter, 131
Jones, Principal, 91
Jordan, M. J., 94
Judd Lumber Co., 19
Judd, Mark, 110,171
Judd, Richard M. Jr., 19
Judd, Richard M. Sr., 77

INDEX

K

Kaiser-Frazer Co., 62
Kauffman, John, 50
Keables, Mrs., 86
Keene, Thomas W., 57
Kellogg, H. F., 72
Kellogg, R. N., 43
Kemp, Candace Spalding, 155
Kendall & Phetteplace, 32
Kimmerle, Grover, 11
Kinnane, James H. 153,213
Klingaman, H. D., 84
Klock, J. N. 44
Knapp, Amos, 71
Knights, Golden Circle, 136

L

Ladies Library Assn. 15,99
Laird, S. B., 88
Lake Dowagiac, 11
Lake, Frank, 49,50,51
Lamoreaux, Maurine, 220
Lardner, Ring, 98
Larzelere, Arthur, 157
Larzelere, Daniel, 34,94
Larzelere, F. G., 34
Larzelere, Harry, 157
Larzelere, Mary Bock, 157
Larzelere, H. E., 108
LaSalle, 22
Leader, U. P., 109
Lee, Anna, 87
Lee, Fred, 34,45,61,68,100
Lee, Henry, 34,57
Lee, Kate Beckwith, 62
Lenning, Mrs. Gil, 127
Letts, John, 136,137
Lewis, R. A., 45
Lillie, Josie, 96
Lincoln, Abraham, 41,152, 170,186
Lincoln, Robert P., 78
Lindsley Lumber Co., 49,50
Lindsley, Victor, 49,50

Lippincott, Sarah Clarke, 16, 149,170
Lockwood, Belva, 83
Lockwood, Mr., 51
Lofland, Joshua, 33,38,43
Lowman, Thornton, 35
Lybrook, Henley C., 33
Lyle, C. E., 72
Lyle, Daniel, 19,72,88,94,106, 145
Lyle, Frank, 45,72
Lyle, Leon, 49,50,51
Lyle, Mary, 99
Lyon, William F., 121

M

Mansfield, Richard, 56
Mantell, Robert, 56,179
Marlowe, Julia, 56
Marr, Dr., 173
Martin, "Fabe," 152,183
Martin, E. C., 79
Martin, Hank, 137
Martin, Thos., 151,169,173
Martin, William, 151
Marx Brothers, 57
Mayhew, Ira, 90
Mayhew, Stella, 57
McAlpine, Frank, 176
McCormick, Samuel, 115
McCue, William, 46
McCullough, John, 179
McElroy, Libbie, 88
McIntosh, Albert, 49
McKee, Supt. 24
McKenzie, Fred, 220
McKenzie, Jim, 220
McKeyes, Horace, 159
McKeyes, Maria Gage, 159
McMaster, Dr. H.S., 72,203
McNair, Mattie, 96
McNair, Spencer, 115
McOmber, Daniel, 17,134,167
McOmber, James, 14,132,164
McOmber, Jay W., 151
Meacham, Charles, 147

INDEX

Mead, A. R., 93
Meek, Richard C., 97
Merwin, Clarence, 107
Merwin, Katy, 57
Metcalf, H. Marie, 90
Michigan Central, 14,17,30,
59,117
Miller, J. R., 88
Miller, Webb, 216
Modjeska, Helene, 56
Moon, Abner, 44,72,79,114,
122,137,205
Moon, Don, 53,220
Moore, Charles, 117
Moore, George, 117,120
Moore, William, 117
Moore, Wm. C. Farm, 179
Morlan, Joseph, 147
Morley, E. D., 106
Morse, Dr. C. W., 204
Morse, Victor, 109
Morse, M. E., 72
Mosher, Francis J., 34,123
Mosher, Ira, 88,163
Mosier, Tom, 220
Muffley, Adam, Jacob, John,
163
Mulvane, Dr. P. S., 204
Mulvane, Mrs. P. S., 99
Munjoy, Charles, 109
Munson, John, 147
Murray and Mack, 56

N

Ndowagayuk, 24
Nansen, Friedhof, 65
Neff, D. L., 49
Neff, Dr. Robert, 34
Neville, John, 134
Niles, 12, 90
Norworth, Jack, 56

O

Oak St. School, 92

Oakley, William, 115
Ober, George, 57
O'Donoghue, John, 104
Old Mill Farm, 155
Onen, Den, 108
Onen, James, 103
Ohio Street, 15
Oppenheim Store, 19,34
Oppenheim, Mark, 19,110
Oppenheim, Maurice, 19,34
Orphan Train, 117

P

Palmer, Dan, 172
Palmer, Hal, 220
Palmer, Maria, 99
Park Place, 17
Parkison, William, 115
Pattison, Edwin, 32
Pattison, Mary, 96
Peck, G. I., 34
Penrod, Georgia, 49
Pickett's Hill, 188
Pine Street, 15
Pipestone, 14,213
Phetteplace, 32
Phillips, Rev. Joseph, 97
Phillipsons, 19,28,33
Platt, Emmet, 46
Poe, Kenneth M., 136
Pokagon, Leopold, 22
Pokagon, Simon, 210
Pompey, Homer, 220
Pond, Ed, 108
Poore, Bolivar, 17
Potawatomi Indians, 22,24,
125,171,205,213
Potter, Frank & Ray, 166
Potter, Noadiah, 166
Power, Frederick, 56,57
Powell Hotel, 166
Price, Chas. K. Jr., 136
Price, Rev. Jacob, 97
Prindle, Dr. C. P. 188,204
Pruess Bakery, 35
Putnam, Uzziel Jr., 132

R

Rail, Angeline, 214
Ramsay, A. G., 34
Randall, Wesley C., 146
Rapp, George, 137
Red Mill, 158
Red Onion Saloon, 27
Red Ruin Saloon, 27
Redner Grocery, 46,219
Redfield, Alexander, 85
Reed, Dr. E. B., 204
Reed, Lyle, 109
Reed, Roland, 56
Mlle. Rhea, 55
Renesten, Mary, 37,155
Renesten, William, 13,18,37, 154,155,161
ReShore, Don B., 110,211
ReShore, Frank, 110,173
ReShore, Gertrude, 99
ReShore, Louis, 34,84
Reynolds, Perry, 108
Riley, James, 133,134
Ritter, Dr. Jesse, 18,154
Rix, John, 116
Rix, Maria Heazlit, 186
Rix, Dr. Thos. G., 204
Robison, Art, 108
Robinson, John W. 146
Robinson, Ransom, 116
Roe, Jesse G., 43
Rose, Mr. Mrs. Virgil, 121
Rosemeier, Mae, 221
Round Oak, 19,57,60,62,66,69, 71,107,111,126
Rouse, Dr. L. V., 204
Root, B. F., 186
Rudolphi, Arthur, 46,55,108
Rudy, 219
Rummel, Daniel, 108
Russey, James, 116

S

St. Alban's, 84
St. Mary's, 12

St. Paul's, 83,93,97,186
Savage, Henry, 123
Scofield, Harry, 109
Schermerhorn, B.J. 176
Schultz, Robert, 130
Scovil, Hiram, 108
Shavehead, 22
Secor, Anthony, 138
Selleck, James, 85
Sherwood, C. L., 19
Sherwood, Mary, 99
Showerman, Ed, 108
Silver Cornet Band, 115
Simmons, Abbie, 87
Simmons, J. W. 88
Simpson, Elias, 163
Simpson, Wm., 138,139
Skinner, Otis, 56
Slater, Prof., 173
Smead, Hattie, 94
Smith, A. J., 142
Smith, Judge Andrew, 174
Smith, Charles A., 43
Smith, Clyde, 108
Smith, Darwin, 115
Smith, Rev. E. P., 119
Smith, Ezekiel, 33
Smith, Harsen D., 174
Smith, Joel H., 32,102,131,150
Smith, M. W., 88
Smith, Sanford, 131
Smith, Wm. Alden, 175,199
Snyder, Maggie, 96
Solf's Bakery, 219
Sojourner Truth, 29
Soules, Peter, 116
Sousa, John Philip, 56
SW Mich. College, 62
Sprague, Bert, 57
Sprague, Hattie Clarke, 57
Sprague, William, 43
Spalding, E. H., 35,37,155
Spalding, Lyman, 37,155
Spalding Mill, 19
Spencer, Amelia
Spencer, James, 88,141
Spicer, George, 134
Spoor, E. H., 44
Starkweather, Ira, 88,185

INDEX

Stebbins, Dr. S.S., 204
Stebbins, Theodore, 34
Steel Furnace Co., 62
Stewart, Will, 109
Stoll, Mrs. Sabrina, Mary, 185
Stover, Lester, 70
Straub, Henry, 173
Sturr, Jacob, 34,134
Sturr, Joseph, 134
Sullivan, Clara, 96
Sullivan, James, 141
Summerell, William, 15
Swank, Millard, 116

T

Tabor, Lester A., 174
Taylor, Halbert, 145,146
Taylor, Tom, 220
Telephone, 45
Thomas, Nellie, 87
Thomas, Mary, 96
Thompson, Denman, 56
Thompson, Prof., 173
Tice, Talmadge, 108
Times, Dowagiac, 79
Topash, Stephen, 213
Topinabee, 125
Tower, C. O., 88
Townsend, Abram, 33,122
Townsend, William, 134
Tri-Co. Telephone Co., 48
Tryon, John, 173
Tryon, Mrs. Spafford, 99
Tryon, Spafford, 173
Turner, George B., 122
Tuthill, Annie, 169
Tuthill, Cyrus, 88
Tuthill, Harry, 169
Tuthill & Sturgis, 33
Tuttle, Harry, 71
Tuttle, William, 71,81

U

Union School, 58,87,92
Union Telephone Co., 48
Universalist Church, 28,83,93, 97,160,186

V

Van Antwerp, Rit, 116
Van Antwerp, Sylvia, 150
Van Buren, A.D.P., 87,90,91
Van Buren Telephone Co. 48
Vanderhoof, Emma, 96
Van Riper, Emma, 99
Van Uxem, A., 33
Veach, Eli, 85
Vaughn, Rev. S.H.D., 97
Vrooman, Belle, 94
Vrooman, C. W., 72

W

Wall, A.C., 94
Wall, Frances, 88
Walter, Rozilla, 96
Walters, Bert, 109
Wares, Fannie, 150
Wares, Loren, 72
Warner, J.P., 71,72
Watson, Robert, 17,123
Ward School, 58
Webb, Capt., 133
Webster, J.A., 44
Weesaw, Winchester, 212
Welch, Orrin T., 87
Weller, Robert J., 100
Wells, Mr. Mrs. Chas., 125
Wells, Henry C., 88,177
Wells, Isaac, 17,125
Wernicke, Julius, 120
Wernicke, Maleta, 121
Wheeler, James, 71,173
Wheeler, Dr. J. H., 204
Wheeler, Minnie, 186
Wheeler, Shepard, 71
White, Dan, 46

INDEX

Whiteley, Harry H., 43
Whiteside, Walker, 56
Whitman, Marcus, 167
Whitney, C. L., 94
Whittier, 16
Wigwam, 41
Wilbur, G. S., 81,94
Wiley, James P., 146
Willard, Frances, 202
Williams, Michael, 24
Winchester, Joseph, 22
Witherell, Thode, 164
Woodhull, Victoria, 83
Wooster, W.M., 44
Wright, Dennis, 13
Wright, Stephen, 156

Y

Young Ladies Seminary, 87,
90
Young Men's Hall, 28